Philippi: How Christianity Began in Europe

Philippi: How Christianity Began in Europe

The Epistle to the Philippians and the Excavations at Philippi

Eduard Verhoef

B L O O M S B U R Y

LONDON • NEW DELHI • NEW YORK • SYDNEY

Bloomsbury T&T Clark
An imprint of Bloomsbury Publishing Plc

50 Bedford Square	175 Fifth Avenue
London	New York
WC1B 3DP	NY 10010
UK	USA

www.bloomsbury.com

First published 2013

British Library Cataloguing-in-Publication Data
A catalogue record for this book is available from the British Library.

ISBN: HB: 978-0-567-42116-6
PB: 978-0-567-33104-5

Library of Congress Cataloging-in-Publication Data
A catalogue record for this book is available from the Library of Congress.

Typeset by Fakenham Prepress Solutions, Fakenham, Norfolk NR21 8NN
Printed and bound in India

CONTENTS

PREFACE

I have been to Greece many times. It is the most beautiful country I know. I always feel at home there and I have often walked there. I travelled on foot from Philippi to Thessalonica, the modern Thessaloniki. Both cities are situated in the north of Greece. Because of my love of Greece, my long walking trips there and because of my study of the Pauline epistles, I was fascinated more and more by the Christian communities that grew up in Philippi and in Thessalonica in the middle of the first century CE. Can we form an idea of the life of these people? How were these communities faring following Paul's death?

In this publication I will constrain myself to the congregation, the church of Philippi. I tried to form a more clear picture of the small group of Philippian people who had answered Paul's message. I registered in photographs many items that are still visible in the ancient Philippi. I collected information about life in Philippi in the following centuries, and in this way I gained insight into the growth process of the ecclesiastic congregation there.

Some of the photographs in this book have been taken by myself. For other photographs I am indebted to Jan D. van der Helm and to my wife, Mariet van Nes. Mrs J. W. van Arenthals MA, Mrs P. C. van Yperen and Drs. G. M. Knepper scrutinized the manuscript. I am most grateful to them for their useful remarks.

Finally, I would like to say how much I enjoyed conducting this research. It is great to finish such a project, but I will contribute follow the new developments there as far as possible. Every year there are excavations on a modest scale, but there are plans as well to start excavations on a broad scale in the western part of Philippi. Who knows what will come to the surface then?

Eduard Verhoef

INTRODUCTION

Paul visited Philippi in the middle of the first century CE. He was able to interest a dozen people in his message. He seems to have revisited the Philippians on at least two occasions. At the beginning of the sixties he wrote an epistle to them: the well-known epistle of Paul to the Philippians. Various matters are discussed in this epistle, from which it is clear that there is some sort of organization of the congregation at that time, because it mentions in Phil. 1.1 that there are bishops and deacons.

In this publication I would like to outline the history of the Christian congregation of Philippi from the time of Paul until approximately the year 600, as far as this is possible with the available data. I will include the civilian community because there are clearly many connections between the civilian community and the ecclesiastical congregation. Such an outline evidently has a tentative character. More data may be found in the future. Under the auspices of the University of Thessaloniki more research is done every year in the eastern part of Philippi, i.e. the area between the Octagon and the eastern city wall. There are also plans to excavate the western part of the ancient town that has not yet been exposed. This will be done under the direction of the Greek Ministry of Culture. But these plans have been postponed time and again. It could take a long time before new excavations will really get started, and I decided not to wait any longer and to report on my findings. I chose the year 600 as the upper limit, because Philippi decayed very quickly at the beginning of the seventh century, when a heavy earth-quake destroyed many buildings. Moreover, raids from the north made life in Philippi more and more difficult. Because of these events ever more people moved away from Philippi and consequently the town was depopulated in the course of several centuries.

My research over many years helped me to attain a more detailed image of Philippi, of the history of the town, and especially of the history of the early Christian congregation. Who were the Philippians? In what type of area did they live? How did they make a living? Was Philippi a big city or only a small town? Were the people indigenous or were there people from other countries as well? If so, what was the proportion of indigenous people to foreigners? Which people did Paul contact? His first visit was presumably followed by two or more (see Acts 20.1-6) and he received support from this congregation in various ways (see Phil. 2.25; 4.15). How were members of the congregation faring following Paul's death, when he could no longer advise and assist them? What happened in the second century and after? Was this small congregation capable of maintaining itself among people with other views? Did the church of Philippi grow? Can we obtain an image of the history of the ecclesiastical congregation in this way? First, I would like to state that it is impossible to answer all of these separate questions, but it has turned out to be possible to form an overall picture of the history of the church of Philippi on the basis of ancient writings, such as Paul's Epistle to the Philippians, the Book of Acts and other documents, and on the basis of inscriptions and archaeological finds.

Philippi is situated about 150 kilometres east of Thessalonica. Most travellers will leave for Philippi from Thessalonica, but it is also possible to fly to Kavala and visit Philippi from there. Thessalonica itself is worth a trip and a thick book. Remnants of buildings from the first centuries CE may be admired in the city centre. Trips to the archaeological museum and especially to the new Byzantine museum prove most rewarding. But it is evident that this city must fall outside the scope of this book. On the way from Thessalonica to Philippi one passes through Amphipolis, a town that Paul visited as well when he made the opposite journey on his way from Philippi to Thessalonica (Acts 17.1; see Map 1, plate section). It is very worthwhile to spend a day in Amphipolis. Its small but excellent museum and its acropolis are usually visited by people who take the trouble to make a detour to Amphipolis. However, the views of the extensive excavations on the west side of the town, down by the River Strymon, are usually overlooked, as are the impressive extant city walls and the remnants of an ancient bridge from the fifth century BCE. Philippi is situated about 60 kilometres to the east of Amphipolis.

In the summer of 1990 I had the opportunity to spend more than a few hours there for the first time. Philippi lay at the foot of the acropolis in the sweltering heat. The acropolis was a hill that could serve as refuge in case of war. Far away, in the southwest, I could see the high Pangaion mountains. Philippi is only an excavation area. Therefore I stayed in the only hotel in the neighbouring village. Both the village and the hotel are called 'Lydia', after the 'seller of purple' who is mentioned in Acts 16. From my comfortable hotel room I could see the peaks of the Pangaion mountains that may be capped with snow according to the season. I conducted research in this area for a number of years. I often spent time in Philippi; I worked in libraries in the north of Greece, and I spoke with scholars who do archaeological research in Philippi and with experts who study the inscriptions that were found there. In this way I tried to obtain an outline of the history of this small congregation. It was a hunt in a very literal sense. I often found doors closed, and it was apparent that nobody knew of inscriptions that were supposed to be located in certain churches.

In other cases my research led to very lucky finds. Once my wife and I were looking for an inscription from the first or second century in the church at the graveyard of Angista. Some freed slaves had it made for their former master. I had nearly lost heart when a priest arrived on a moped. In my best Greek I asked him if he knew of this inscription. With a large gesture he invited us in and brought us to the door that gave entrance to the altar. Greek Orthodox law forbids women from entering at this point, and accordingly my wife was left standing there, but I was allowed in. As the priest was donning his vestment he pushed a table aside and rolled up an old carpet, and revealed the inscription I was looking for, right before the altar. It was very easy to read, stating that the freedman Gaius Firmius and his sons Gaius Firmius, Sextus Firmius and Lucius Firmius had this inscription made for their master (Figure 1). Such an inscription does not provide much information, certainly not about the early Christian church in this area, but it confirms the impression that from the beginning of the common era slaves were sometimes liberated in the Roman Empire. These freedmen could then forge a living of their own, however problematic this may have been. Freedmen would often thank their master for their liberation and have an inscription made to that effect.

People who are well versed in the Bible will probably be familiar with the epistle of Paul to the Philippians. The Christ Hymn (Phil. 2.6-11) is well known and Hymn 225 from the Church Hymnary is based on these verses. At the end of this book I provide the translation of this epistle as it has been published in the New Revised Standard Version (NRSV). In my opinion the Epistle to the Philippians is a coherent whole, and not, as some scholars propose, a compilation of several epistles. Other points under discussion are the place and the time of origin of this epistle. In my view the strongest arguments support the conclusion that Paul wrote this epistle when he was in prison in Rome shortly after the year 60. I also include parts of the Book of Acts that are very relevant within the scope of this book: Acts 16.11–17.1 and Acts 20.1-6. All parts of the Bible cited in this book are from the New Revised Standard Version.

1

The earliest history of Philippi

The area where the town of Philippi is situated was inhabited several centuries before the beginning of the Common Era. This is not surprising, since this location provided many advantages. Neapolis (today Kavala) was only 15 kilometres away and it had a spacious and sheltered harbour. The very fertile soil was easy to work. The luxuriant vegetation was so well known that Theophrastes, a follower of Aristotle, stayed there several times to study it at the end of the fourth century BCE. He wrote several books on plants, and mentioned as a peculiarity of this area that the willows were successfully pollarded. He discussed the cultivation of broad beans here and he admired the many beautiful roses. He noticed that the frost had become less harmful than before, because the water level in the marshland had fallen, which left more land for cultivation.

The acropolis at the north side of the plain offered a comfortable opportunity to oversee the whole area. In case of danger people could retreat to the acropolis and defend themselves there. The fact that there was marshland in the south contributed to the favourable conditions, as this territory could be approached only from the west and the east. Consequently the town could not be raided unnoticed. However, centuries later it would become clear that in the long run these circumstances could not provide enough safety against attacks from the northwest.

The inhabitants of the island of Thasos near the coast close to Kavala had recognized the value of the area. They conquered it in 360 BCE and founded a town there which they called Krenides. It was the precursor of the later Philippi. The Thasians for their part were threatened by Thracian tribes from the northeast and they asked Philip II, King of Macedonia and father of Alexander the Great, for help. Philip II, realizing the major strategic value of the town, was more than willing to meet their request. The silver and gold-mines in the nearby Pangaion mountains represented economic value as well. Therefore Philip II came to this area with his armies at the request of the inhabitants, probably in 356 BCE, in order to protect them against the pillaging of the Thracians. He added the whole area as far as the river Nestos to his kingdom. He then founded a new town to the west of Krenides, bringing people of various settlements together, and built a wall around it. Ancient sources say that Philip had many people settle here, but it is unclear how many people were involved. Contrary to this assumption, it must have been a town of modest size. It was called 'Philippi' after its founder. From this time on coins were minted in Philippi bearing the name of Philip.

The inhabitants of Philippi were largely Greeks from Thasos, Macedonians, and to a lesser extent Thracians from the north and the northeast. These were joined by migrants from Egypt, Asia Minor, Israel and other countries. Texts, inscriptions and archaeological finds testify to this.

Large parts of the city walls may be seen even today, though the Romans later built several new sections on the ancient foundations. The oldest parts may be identified in the large rectangular blocks of different sizes. An ancient part has been preserved where the wall and the theatre meet (Figure 2). The city wall had three gates. There was the so-called Neapolis Gate in the east wall, a gate set in the south wall which has been called the Marsh Gate in modern literature, and there was a gate in the west section, close to the village of Lydia, which was the point of departure for travellers to the west. It is often called the Krenides Gate in the literature, but this name is confusing because the village of Krenides is situated to the east of Philippi. Some parts of the Neapolis Gate remain standing today.

People travelling from the present village of Krenides to the theatre in Philippi see the city wall and the Neapolis Gate as they approach. The theatre is located slightly north of the road. It was built in the time of Philip II. In spite of the fact that the Romans rebuilt and enlarged it in later times, some parts of it date from Philip's time, including the eastern connection with the city wall. It is only possible to draw an approximate map of the ancient Hellenistic Philippi. The Romans rebuilt the town completely. Consequently, the earlier street pattern cannot be indicated with any certainty. However, the location of the city walls is certain. The remnants of the Neapolis Gate and of the west gate make it probable that the Via Egnatia was constructed on the trajectory of an earlier road. The Via Egnatia led through the town from the west gate to the Neapolis Gate. Most Philippians lived to the south of the Via Egnatia, on the plain section of the walled area. The shops and public buildings were located here as well.

A short time after Philip II, his son Alexander the Great became involved with Philippi. His decision was required on border disputes between the inhabitants of Philippi and the Thracians. The Thracians had been defeated by Philip, but apparently they continued to challenge the exact location of the borders in this area. Alexander's decree weighs the interests of both parties and carefully describes the northern border of the territory of Philippi. The stone with the chiselled text of this decree may now be seen in the museum in Philippi.

The Philippians travelled to other parts of the then known world. Inscriptions from Samothrace, for example, mention that people from Philippi stayed there. Contacts with other Greek cities are mentioned as well. Inscriptions have been found that tell us about Philippians taking part in national competitions. Several inscriptions have been discovered in Delphi that list participants in contests, in which Philippians apparently often participated. The results of these competitions are not mentioned in these inscriptions. The Philippians must undoubtedly have had hopes that their representatives would win, but it would take some time before they heard the results; the distance between Delphi and Philippi is about 500 kilometres. Philippians are also named on lists of people who made donations to temples in cities such as Argos and Delphi. Such inscriptions confirm that Philippi was known in the wider area in spite of the fact that is was not a large or important city.

Little is known about the history of Philippi in the first centuries following its foundation. The wars between the Romans and the

Macedonians cannot have passed unnoticed, but we do not have any information about Philippi during these wars. What we do know is that in 168 BCE the Roman general Lucius Aemilius Paullus won a definitive victory over the Macedonians. Macedonia was divided into four districts, each with its own capital. Amphipolis became the capital of the east district which included Philippi, located approximately between the rivers Strymon and Nestos. The capitals of the other districts were Thessalonica, Pella and Pelagonia. This zoning into districts did not last long. A revolt by the Macedonians twenty years later, in 148 BCE, caused the Romans to consolidate the four districts into one large province together with Epiros in the west of Greece. Thessalonica became the capital of the entire area, but the division into districts continued to exist in common parlance. It is clear from Acts 16.12 that the author of the Book of Acts was well informed about this old division. Contrary to what many translations say, the author wrote: a town of the first district.

Around this time the Romans started constructing the main road which would eventually connect Dyrrhachium in present Albania at the Adriatic Sea with Byzantium, present-day Istanbul. This road was called the Via Egnatia after Gnaeus Egnatius, who started to build it. It led to the southeast from Dyrrhachium to Thessalonica. In the time of Emperor Augustus it ran further in an easterly direction via Amphipolis, Angista, Kalambaki and Philippi to Byzantium. We can walk on some parts of this road even today. A part of it may be seen close to Kavala (Figure 3). The old Roman Via Egnatia is quite straight and steep. A few metres to the east a winding road has been constructed for the cars that drive up the mountain, which separates the Philippian plain from Kavala. In Philippi people can walk on the Via Egnatia as well, for example, north of the forum. It must have been a difficult job to lay the bulky and heavy stones. Milestones indicated the distances that had to be crossed to reach important towns or cities. An older milestone has recently been found in Kalambaki, a village not far from Philippi. It is preserved in the museum of Drama. It indicates that the distance to Philippi is 30 stadia, about 5.5 kilometres (Figure 4). The distance from Amphipolis is indicated on the reverse, but unfortunately this side has been damaged.

Scholars have calculated that the trip from Rome to Byzantium by the Via Egnatia took about 24 days. To a large extent this journey was made overland. The advantages were clear: it could be travelled during the whole year and it was less dangerous than the trip across the sea. On the other hand, the overland trip was much slower. It is clear that the Via Egnatia was very important for a town such as Philippi. As travelling to other cities became much easier, this road saw a steep increase in commercial traffic. On the other hand, the Roman legions also used this road on their way to the east, and this must have frightened the Philippians. The Roman general Lucius Valerius Flaccus, for example, passed Philippi in 86 BCE on his way to do battle against Mithridates, a regional leader who intended to found a country of his own in Asia Minor. The internal tensions in the Roman Empire increased during this period, and in such problematic situations it was possible for soldiers to seize the first opportunity to plunder. After all, the right to plunder was often part of the soldiers' payment. It is easy to imagine that the inhabitants of Philippi watched the movements of the troops with trepidation.

The Via Egnatia needed to be kept in good repair over the centuries, but the Romans did not always carry out the necessary maintenance. An inscription on one milestone that is now in the museum of Drama makes mention of deferred maintenance and of repairs carried out by the order of Emperor Trajan (98–117 CE).

In the first century BCE an important battle was fought on the territory of Philippi. The Roman Empire had increased enormously, and became involved in a civil war in the middle of the first century BCE. Octavian, later known as Augustus, and Mark Antony adopted wider powers and formed a triumvirate with Lepidus. The triumvirate wielded virtually dictatorial power. The role of Lepidus was quite minor, but Octavian and Mark Antony made a stand against the republicans Brutus and Cassius. A decisive battle was fought in 42 BCE on the plain of Philippi, at the foot of the acropolis. Brutus and Cassius were defeated on 23 October of the year 42 BCE, and according to some authors their defeat here constituted the end of the Roman Republic.

Due to illness shortly before and during this battle, Octavian had barely been able to participate in this struggle. In his memoirs Octavian claims the victory for himself, but this is historically incorrect. Mark Antony's name is not even mentioned, though he undoubtedly played the more important role. After this battle Mark Antony decided to subject Philippi to the direct rule of Rome and to make it a Roman colony. Coins minted in Philippi in this time bear the letters A I C V P, which is an abbreviation for *Antonii Iussu Colonia Victrix Philippensium*: by order of Antony, the victorious colony of the Philippians. The word *victrix*, victorious, obviously refers to the battle here that was won by Mark Antony. Other Roman colonies include Pella, to the west of Thessalonica, and Dyrrhachium, where the Via Egnatia was begun.

It was decided that a large number of veterans should be settled in Philippi, and their presence created a buffer zone against any enemy raids. This settlement of veterans fulfilled another purpose as well. Veterans usually performed military service for more than 20 years. When they were discharged they were given a plot of land so that they became self-supporting. The size of such a parcel of land differed with the various colonies. We know of examples of about 30 acres that were given to ordinary soldiers. Those of a superior rank received a much larger piece of land. There were specific rituals involved in the granting of land. First, land surveyors pegged out parcels in the town and its surroundings. Then two priests drove a plough, pulled by a bull and a cow. The furrows thus created defined the land. After the ritual with the plough, lots were drawn by an official, and the parcels were granted accordingly. This ritual is visible on certain coins from Philippi and other Roman colonies. The obverse shows a portrait of Emperor Augustus, and the reverse shows two priests with a cow and a bull (see Figure 5).

Large amounts of land were was needed for the discharged soldiers. The people living on the land were often compelled to leave, but they were sometimes given the opportunity to lease the land. The veterans thus had a source of income which did not require much effort. It must have been the same in Philippi. The territory belonging to the colony of Philippi was very large, as were the territories of other colonized areas. Colonies could accommodate many immigrants without incurring any major problems. Philippi had authority over several villages in the surrounding area. Some colonists may have elected to live a little further from Philippi, where there was more space than near Philippi.

The territory of Philippi extended for about 2,000 square kilometres. The Symvolo mountains to the south and the Falakro mountains to the north constituted the borders of Philippi's territory. In the west the villages of Podochori and Angista belonged to the territory of Philippi, and the eastern border ran from Neapolis, now known as Kavala, almost due north. It is evident that many colonists could obtain a piece of land here, but most may have settled in Philippi and its immediate vicinity. For other cities with colonists Roman authors mention numbers varying from a few hundred to several thousands of newcomers. With respect to Philippi the number is probably 1,000 or more.

Philippi was increasingly Romanized. The local administration was organized after the Roman model with *duumviri*, literally (commission of) *two men*. This title was given to two equal magistrates who governed the town together. The most important offices were taken by Roman citizens. The situation in Thessalonica, however, was quite different. Thessalonica remained a 'free city', though this freedom was rather constrained. Thessalonica had Greek officials who carried out the offices. They had the title of *politarchs*. The author of the Book of Acts was apparently well informed about these different forms of government, because the various offices are rendered correctly in the Greek text of the Book of Acts.

For Mark Antony and Octavian the strategic and economic interest of Philippi was evident. Philippi was valuable with regard to the enduring conflicts with the Thracians in the northeast. In additon, though the silver and gold mines may have been exhausted, the economic value of Philippi had increased since the construction of the Via Egnatia. Philippi benefited from the nearby presence of the harbour of Neapolis. Travel from Philippi to Neapolis was easy, and people could sail from Neapolis to Thasos and beyond.

More than ten years later, in 31 BCE, Mark Antony and Octavian fought each other in the battle of Actium in the west of Greece. Octavian no longer considered Mark Antony reliable. He defeated Mark Antony in this battle and effectively assumed sole power over the immense Roman Empire.

Now it was Octavian who interfered in life in Philippi. He changed the name of the town and called it *Colonia Iulia Augusta Philippensium*: 'the colony of the Philippians of Julius Augustus', after himself. Octavian had adopted the name Julius to honour Julius Caesar, while the honorary name Augustus was granted him by the Senate in 27 BCE. Mark Antony's name was no longer

mentioned on the coins of Philippi. Octavian granted Philippi the
so-called *Ius Italicum*. This meant that Philippi enjoyed the same
legal status as Italian cities, which brought the colony fiscal advantages among other things. Again a number of colonists were forced
to settle in Philippi, but this time some of these were citizens from
the neighbourhood of Rome, former followers of Mark Antony.
Octavian ordered them to leave their grounds and make room for
veterans from Octavian's legions.

In addition, a cohort of praetorians was quartered in Philippi. At
that time a cohort usually consisted of 1,000 men. The praetorian
guard was among the Emperor's elite troops. Coins minted in
Philippi show the regimental standards of the praetorians with the
legend *Cohor(s) Prae(toria) Phil(ippensis)*, the Philippian cohort of
praetorians. Victoria, the goddess of victory, is portrayed on the
obverse of this coin (see Figures 6a and 6b). The legend *Vic(toria)
Aug(usta)* and the image of the goddess lend a religious dimension
to Octavian's victory. Later Octavian was venerated as *divus
Augustus*, the divine August. Even though it is sometimes argued
that these coins were minted only after Augustus' death, this still
means that they are a good illustration of the presence of the
praetorians in Philippi.

As was mentioned above, more Romans had come to Philippi
following the battle near Actium. These groups were probably
larger than the number of colonists that Mark Antony had settled
there. By then the total number of inhabitants of Philippi must have
been nearly 10,000.

The colony of Philippi and its territory were conferred to the
tribus (tribe) Voltinia. Originally a tribus was a district in Rome
or in its vicinity. Such a tribus served as a voting district as well.
Romans living in a certain district belonged to the tribus concerned,
but with the expansion of the Roman Empire an increasing number
of new areas were conferred to a particular tribus. Consequently
areas that were far apart could belong to the same tribus. The
Romans who came to Philippi belonged to the tribus Voltinia
or became members of this tribus. About 70 of the nearly 900
published inscriptions mention this name, abbreviated to *Vol*.
For example, one inscription mentions a certain Sextus Volcasius
who belonged to the tribus Voltinia. He was probably among the
colonists who were sent to Philippi by Mark Antony, shortly after

42 BCE. As he originally came from Pisa he probably once belonged to the tribus Galeria, but as a Roman citizen living in Philippi he became a member of the tribus Voltinia.

Another inscription was made in honour of proconsul Marcus Lollius, son of Marcus. The stone bearing this inscription lies upside down between the ruins to the west of the forum. In this text the less frequent abbreviation *Volt.* is used for the tribus Voltinia (Figure 7). The lower half of the second line has disappeared, but nonetheless we can easily read the text M(arco) Lollio M(arci) F(ilio) Volt, for Marcus Lollius, son of Marcus, from the tribus Voltinia. I have added the usual omissions in brackets. Marcus Lollius' term of office was presumably 12 months, at the end of the first century CE.

Names of other districts were seldom mentioned in Philippi. Paul may have alluded to the pride of the Roman citizens in Philippi in belonging to the tribus Voltinia when he said in Phil. 3.20 with respect to the Christians: 'But our citizenship is in heaven.' He may have deliberately opposed their Voltinian citizenship with their citizenship in heaven.

There must have been an official list with the names of Romans who belonged to the tribus Voltinia. Perhaps Paul was thinking of this list when he mentioned his co-workers in Phil. 4.3 and stated that their 'names are in the book of life', but this is only a possibility. Such a book is mentioned in Ps. 69.29 as well.

It is very difficult to form a clear image of the situation in Philippi following the two influxes of immigrants mentioned above. The Roman newcomers must have been considered as representatives of the occupying force. Tensions were bound to rise, but we do not know anything about this. When Roman legions marched over the Via Egnatia the Greeks must have looked on with sorrow, while the Romans may have watched them with approval. In 20 BCE Tiberius, who would later become emperor, marched over the Via Egnatia to Philippi with his legions on his way to the territory of the Armenians. It is certain that the Philippians were not happy with such incidents, but the Romans were definitely in control.

Another radical change following the arrival of the two groups of Romans was that most people now spoke Latin, especially the officials. The inscriptions dated in the first centuries CE show that Latin would remain the official language for several centuries. A large bath house was built for the immigrants, the ruins of which are clearly visible north of the so-called Octagon (see Plan 1, plate section). Parts of the trajectory of the water pipes show us the rooms where hot water was available. The veterans lived on land that had earlier been inhabited by Greeks or Macedonians. The arable land was used for growing crops as well as for breeding livestock. Doubtless many veterans allowed slaves or the former owners to farm the land. Naturally, the *duumviri*, the administrators of the town, were Romans. They are mentioned in Acts 16.20. In the original Greek text they are called *strategoi*, strategists. We know the name of some *duumviri*, because their names are mentioned in inscriptions, for example, Publius Cornelius Asper Atiarius Montanus and Varinius Macedo. But there must have been many more than the handful whose names we know, because they were usually appointed for only 12 months. The *lictores*, police officers, immediately answered to the *duumviri*. They were responsible for the implementation of resolutions and for the execution of passed sentences. They also functioned as escort of the *duumviri*. In Acts 16.35 we read that the *lictores* had to take care of the release of Paul and Silas.

Of course many more Romans played a role in the city admin-istration and public life. With some imagination we can form a general idea, which is very difficult to support with concrete evidence however. There were construction activities which required the appointment of inspectors. Priests were appointed, and some enterprising men may have opened shops. One of the problems is that the inscriptions that have remained were usually made by the order of the rich, who could afford to have grave-stones or sarcophagi made and monuments built. The large burial chambers that were found in the village of Krenides belonged to wealthy families as well. Consequently we need to realize that the inscriptions and the archaeological finds always give a one-sided impression. Moreover, the only objects that have remained were made of durable material, and such materials were expensive. There are some inscriptions made by freedmen, for example, but in general we may say that the surviving memorial stones belonged to the well-to-do.

There were various deities venerated in Philippi and the surrounding area. Sources mention as many as 35 different deities. We usually have little information about the manner in which these deities were worshipped, because frequently mysteries were an important part of the cult, and secrecy was often compulsory. However, on the basis of the inscriptions that have been found we can build a rough picture of the religious life in Philippi. The Thracians generally remained loyal to their Thracian Horseman, who was often referred to as Heros Aulonites in inscriptions. Inscriptions dating from the third century BCE have been found with beautiful images of this deity on a galloping horse. But he was often depicted in later times as well. A Greek text below one of these images says that Manta made this memorial for her son and put money at the disposal of the officials for an annual sacrifice. The names on the inscriptions show that the cult of the Thracian Horseman attracted many Greeks and Romans as well, but the majority were Thracians. A sanctuary of the Thracian Horseman has been excavated in Kipia, about 15 kilometres southwest of Philippi. This area once belonged to the territory of Philippi. Animals were sacrificed there and some of their blood was sprinkled on the newly initiated. After this ritual there was a communal feast.

Dionysus was venerated in Philippi and its environs as well. A simple sanctuary in his honour had been built centuries earlier in the Pangaion mountains. A temple for the cult of Dionysus was built in Drama in Hellenistic times. It is said that Dionysus changed his form from a god into a human being as he travelled to Thebes, where his mother had died. This and other stories indicate that the idea of a god who revealed himself in the form of a human being was not unknown to the Philippians. The Christ Hymn in Phil. 2.6-11 comes to mind in this respect, though of course many differences may be mentioned as well. This Christ Hymn tells us that Christ Jesus was equal to God, and took 'the form of a slave, being born in human likeness'. The names of priests of Dionysus are still legible in some inscriptions. It is well known that the use of intoxicants was very important for followers of this cult. The beverages made people forget their misery in divine intoxication, keeping alive the hope of a better future. According to the adherents of this cult their future would hold sheer pleasure. It is clear, then, that the worshippers of Dionysus drank abundantly during their meetings.

After the conquest of the area by the Thasians in 360 BCE other deities were also venerated, such as Apollo and Artemis. We will see that Artemis, called Diana in Latin, attracted huge attention in Philippi in later times.

The new cult of the Roman Emperor was introduced by the Roman colonists shortly after their arrival. Soon the Emperor was even deified. In his memoirs Emperor Augustus mentions the deeds of the *divus Augustus*, the divine August. Later on, emperors were venerated as gods soon after they had taken office. In the first century CE monuments were erected in Philippi in honour of the Caesarean family, and in the second century temples were even built in their honour. Priests were appointed, holidays were instituted and sacrifices to the Emperor were made. Next to the priests the so-called *sexviri Augustales*, the six men working in honour of Augustus, played a role in the cult of the Emperor. They were responsible for organizing the celebrations in honour of the Emperor. All inhabitants could participate in these celebrations.

Many of the less affluent Romans adhered to the cult of the god Silvanus, which they had taken along from Rome. Silvanus was associated with agrarian life, especially with the breeding of livestock, but also with arable farming.

Religions from other countries were also represented alongside these well-known cults, but these religions had fewer followers. Evidence has been found that the Egyptian goddess Isis was worshipped in the second century, but she may have been venerated even earlier. There was no impediment against participation in more than one cult, though the one condition was that the veneration of the Emperor would not suffer at the hands of other cults, because the town was dependent on the Emperor for the common good.

In this regard the cult of a certain Euephenes, son of Exekestos, should be mentioned. His tomb has been found within the city walls. On the basis of inscriptions bearing his name it is quite certain that this Euephenes was a priest of the Kabeiroi, deities who were venerated on the island of Samothrace and somewhat differently in Thessalonica, as well as in Amphipolis. Very seldom was it allowed to bury a person within the city walls. This was done only when a hero was buried, or a person who was venerated as the founder of the city. It is evident, then, that this Euephenes must have played a special role.

The sanctuary containing such a tomb was called the heroon, the memorial shrine of a hero. Such sanctuaries have been excavated in Ephesus and elsewhere. Classical authors tell us that singing, dancing and feasting were important elements of the festivities around similar tombs. The way in which this tomb in Philippi has been built shows that it had a cultic role. A shrine was built above it and there was a precinct around this sanctuary (see Plan 1, plate section). Above the subterranean burial chamber there were three steps to a kind of dais, on which a shrine was erected. Nothing is left of this shrine, but we can easily identify the dais. We do not know the exact role of the shrine with respect to the veneration of Euephenes, but we will discuss later the fact that this cult would endure in Philippi for a long time.

Summarizing, we may say that Philippi had probably nearly 10,000 inhabitants at the beginning of our era. This estimate is based on comparisons with the inhabitable territories of other cities, on the size of the theatre, etc. This population makes the town smaller than Newhaven in East Sussex, for instance, or Sheerness in Kent. Philippi was certainly not a metropolis, not even by the standards of its own time. It is significant that authors in the first centuries wrote about Philippi virtually exclusively with respect to the battle in 42 BCE. Words were hardly ever devoted to the town itself. It did not have many celebrities among its inhabitants. The historian Marsyas and the philosopher Adrastos may be mentioned here, but they are exceptions.

Various nationalities were present in Philippi: there were Greeks from Thasos and from southern Greece, but Macedonians and Romans constituted the majority. There were people from Thracia, Egypt and Asia Minor as well, and perhaps also people from Israel, and more nationalities could certainly be found. The relatively large numbers of Romans had only settled there after the battles at Philippi and Actium, in 42 and 31 BCE respectively.

The workforce was especially concerned with crop farming and stock-breeding. Commerce was important. Quite a large number of people must have worked in stone quarries. Marble was quarried and prepared there for the construction of roads, and for the erection of temples and houses. Stewards supervised the properties of wealthy Romans. A number of people in the working classes would have been slaves. Their number may be estimated at 20 per cent of the entire population. Various religions were represented. The Thracian Horseman, Silvanus and Dionysus probably had the most adherents. And of course the cult of the Roman Emperor was very important.

2

The first century CE: the emergence of a Christian congregation

In the middle of the first century CE Paul, Timothy and Silas walked across the Via Egnatia to travel the 15 kilometres from Neapolis to Philippi. They had just made the crossing from Troas to Neapolis. Having passed Samothrace and Thasos, they were now on their way to Philippi. After crossing the slopes of the Symvolo mountains, they had a view over the vast plain where Philippi was situated.

After the battle in 42 BCE it had remained rather quiet in Philippi. True, legions sometimes marched across the Via Egnatia on their way to the East, but to our knowledge these events had not had dramatic consequences for the town. It appears that sometimes there were skirmishes between the Romans and the Thracians in the north and the northeast, but these clashes did not pose a real threat to Philippi. It was only in 44 and 45 CE that the Romans fought against the Thracians on a larger scale. The Philippians experienced this struggle at first hand and, as was customary, they probably had to contribute towards the costs of the maintenance of the legions that waged a fight in their territory. A year later, in 46 CE, the Thracian king Roemetalkes III was murdered, and subsequently the whole area to the north and northeast of Philippi was without doubt subjected to the rule of the Romans. The relation between the Thracians and the Romans was rather complicated. The Roman Marcus Acculeius had made an inscription in honour of his friend Roemetalkes II, King of Thracia (18–37), which shows his appreciation. We can still see this inscription on the west side of the forum (Figure 8). Both Roemetalkes II and Roemetalkes III were put on the throne through the agency of the Romans. Although they had tried to secure the Roman interests, their people resisted any Roman influence.

The rather large number of Romans that had settled in Philippi had increased the population considerably. We may assume that the number of inhabitants of Philippi had nearly reached 10,000 after the settlement of the two groups of colonists. It is generally accepted that the population of the entire Roman Empire was about 60 million at the beginning of our era and that this number barely increased during the first centuries. Epidemics of plague and wars claimed many victims, which nullified the natural increase in population. For the same reason the number of inhabitants of Philippi probably remained unchanged during in these centuries.

The majority of the inhabitants of Philippi were Greeks by birth, but to a great extent the Romans were decisive for the atmosphere of the town. Most inscriptions were written in Latin. The much larger city of Thessalonica may have been inhabited by nearly 100,000 people, but only a few Romans lived in this 'free city', and only a few Latin inscriptions have been found there. The same is true for a town like Amphipolis. A number of Greek inscriptions have been found there, but only a few inscriptions in Latin. It is remarkable that some inscriptions originating from the territory of Philippi show Latin words written in Greek letters. For example, an inscription in the garden of the museum in Philippi that originates from the first century says that a certain Aliupaibes, son of Zeipalas, had an inscription made on the tomb of his wife Tertia (Figure 9). The same text informs us that a woman called Sekous made money available for an annual sacrifice to the gods. The custom of making an annual sacrifice to the gods in commemoration of the deceased is mentioned more often in inscriptions of that era. The names Aliupaibes and Sekous indicate that these people were Thracians by descent. Apparently Thracians sometimes used Greek letters to express themselves in Latin. Although they could speak Latin, the use of Greek letters was apparently more obvious for them. A Greek inscription from the first century that is rather surprising shows the judgment of a Roman administrator with respect to the Philippian–Thasian border. Apparently it was unclear where the border ran, and this high-ranking Roman official's verdict ruled that he would place the boundary stones himself. But such Greek inscriptions were exceptions, especially when the inscriptions were made by order of Roman officials. The Roman influence was pervasive in Philippi and by far the larger parts of the inscriptions were written in Latin.

The many inscriptions have provided us with the names and sometimes the professions of certain inhabitants of that area. For example, a sarcophagus has been found of an actor from the first century. The inscription tells us with respect to this man, Titus Uttiedius Venerianus, that he had been an actor for 37 years when he died at the age of 75. His wife, Alfena Saturnina, had died at the age of 51, and she had been buried in this sarcophagus as well. Occasionally we can reconstruct the connection between relatives. The name of the earlier-mentioned Publius Cornelius Asper Atiarius Montanus, one of the duumviri from the first century, is still partly legible on a sarcophagus that is now in the garden of the archaeo-logical museum in Kavala. The sarcophagus of his daughter is there as well. She was called Cornelia Asprilla and she died when she was only 35 years old. She was priestess of the deified Empress Livia Augusta, Emperor Augustus' wife. The sarcophagus of the wife of Publius Cornelius Asper should be mentioned here as well. She was called Cornelia Longa and she died at the age of 60. She had probably survived her daughter.

Other tombs suggest very sad events. We read on a gravestone that a certain Publius Veneteius Phoebus, 'our dearest son', was buried there. He was ten years old. Another gravestone, from the first or the second century, mentions that a man had this tomb made for his son Posidonius, who died at the age of 18, and for his wife Susa.

Just east of the village Krenides a stone of nearly 4 metres high was erected that lists the merits of the soldier Gaius Vibius Quartus (Figure 10) who lived in the middle of the first century. The commemorative stone stands by the side of a small road to Kavala. This is the old trajectory of the Via Egnatia. Gaius Vibius Quartus belonged to the tribus Cornelia and served in the fifth

Macedonian legion. It is almost certain that Paul walked along this road as he travelled from Neapolis to Philippi, and he may have passed this stone, which was probably already in place at that time. Another Roman soldier was Lucius Tatinius Cnosus, who is mentioned in several inscriptions. One of these, which may be seen in the northwest corner of the forum, lists his merits. Tatinius had another inscription made, mentioning that he was very thankful for the peace and quiet in Philippi. The first lines are easy to read: *quieti Aug(ustae) Col(oniae) Philippiens(is)* [for the peace and quiet of the Colonia Augusta Philippi] (Figure 11). The former inscription has been damaged. It is striking to see that more than one line has been chipped off, which was almost certainly the name of Emperor Domitian. This emperor (81–96) had made so many enemies through his high-handed actions that people wanted to erase him from memory after his violent death.

Another profession that is sometimes mentioned in the inscriptions is that of munerarius, whose task it was to organize games. Just south of the forum, where the shops used to be, we can read an inscription that mentions a certain Varinius Macedo. He performed the duty of munerarius twice. We saw earlier that he was one of the two duumviri in this century.

The northeast corner of the forum still features the enormous blocks that served as pedestals for the (probably) seven statues of priestesses for Livia Augusta. Their names are partially preserved. On the bottom line it reads: *Maecia C(ai) f(ilia) Auruncina Calaviana fecit* [Maecia Auruncina Calaviana, the daughter of Gaius, erected this] (Figure 12). It must have been an huge monument in remembrance of these women, who had placed their lives in the service of the veneration of the Empress. The construction workers must have experienced great difficulties when putting the heavy blocks in place. We saw earlier that a priestess of Livia Augusta was mentioned on a sarcophagus that is preserved in the garden of the museum in Kavala.

On the basis of these findings it is clear that Philippi had a pervasive Roman atmosphere when Paul arrived there in 49 or 50. For many people Latin was the common language, and several typically Roman functions were called into existence. Paul had used the common route: from Troas in Asia Minor he had sailed to the seaport of Neapolis (Acts 16.11), now Kavala, which was situated about ten miles from Philippi. The Via Egnatia connected these towns, and this road provided a good way to travel further to other cities in the west. Paul came ashore here with Silas and Timothy, and they walked together on the Via Egnatia. It seems that Paul did not intend to stay in Neapolis, but intended to travel immediately to the Roman colony of Philippi. Having visited several Roman colonies in Asia Minor as well, Paul seems to have had a preference for staying at Roman colonies. As the travellers passed by the enormous stone of Gaius Vibius Quartus (if this memorial was already there), they would have seen the acropolis. From this location it would have taken them about 30 minutes to reach the city wall. They did not know the town. Everything was new to them, and nothing suggests that they could rely on any acquaintances.

On the sabbath they went outside the gate to a place by the river, assuming there would be a place of prayer for the Jews there. This was the most logical starting point for Paul. He had the same background and he could try to join in the tradition they shared. The fact that Paul and his co-workers went to look for a place of prayer indicates that there was not yet a synagogue in Philippi. A synagogue is only mentioned in an inscription that is dated from the third or fourth century. Paul probably left the town close to the so-called Marsh Gate. He could not have used the western gate, sometimes called Krenides Gate, because it led further outside the town than the Jews were allowed to walk on the sabbath according to the Jewish laws. The large cemetery there makes it very improbable as well that the Jews would have met at this place of all places for their prayers. We can still see some of the gravestones at this burial site. Nevertheless, a new baptistery has recently been built outside the Krenides Gate, and various religious ceremonies are celebrated there nowadays.

On this particular sabbath they met a dealer in purple cloth, Lydia. Her name tells us that she was a woman from Lydia, a district in Asia Minor. Acts 16.14 informs us that she was from the city of Thyatira, a town north of Smyrna, present-day Izmir. In this area of Asia Minor purple was an important trading product and the purple of this area was traded in large parts of the Roman Empire at the time. This material was very precious, and only high Roman officials had been allowed to wear certain purple adornments since the middle of the first century. Lydia may have had connections in high Roman circles because of her trade.

The greetings from the people of Caesar's household in Phil. 4.22 may have been connected with Lydia's contacts with Roman dignitaries. In this respect it is interesting that an inscription reads that Cadmus, Atimetus and Martialis, three slaves who were freed by Emperor Augustus, mention that they had a monument built in honour of the Emperor. They also belonged to Caesar's household in a broader sense. This inscription may be seen in the western part of Basilica B; the stone is leaning against the wall (Figure 13). With the help of such inscriptions it is very easy to establish the Roman influence on life in Philippi. It is also clear that the Epistle to the Philippians has more common ground with the Roman world than any other Pauline epistle.

Lydia is said to be the first convert in Philippi; but others soon followed, according to Phil. 1.5, where Paul speaks to the Philippians about their 'sharing in the gospel from the first day until now'. On the basis of texts in the Book of Acts and in the Epistle to the Philippians we can trace a number of these converts. A slave girl who had 'a spirit of divination' is mentioned in Acts 16.16, but we are not told that she complied with Paul's message. Paul's behaviour towards this slave girl led to a disturbance, and as a consequence Paul and Silas were beaten with rods and thrown into prison; cf. 1 Thess. 2.2. Following the miraculous events which occurred that very night the goaler on duty was convinced of the truth of Paul's words, and he and his entire family were baptized; Acts 16.33. The Book of Acts describes two more visits by Paul to Philippi; these are mentioned in Acts 20.1-2, and Acts 20.6. These visits took place before Paul was brought to Rome as a prisoner and consequently before the Epistle to the Philippians was written. Meanwhile the congregation in Philippi had increased considerably. The Epistle to the Philippians was written shortly after the year 60. In it more people are mentioned than in Acts, though not always by name. Bishops and deacons are mentioned in Phil. 1.1. The plural form makes us conclude that there were at least two bishops and two deacons at the time.

Paul mentions a certain Epaphroditus in Phil. 2.25-30. Apparently this Epaphroditus had been sent to Paul by the Philippians to help him out of his hopeless situation in prison, but a serious illness had made it impossible for him to perform this task. According to Phil. 2.28 Paul sent Epaphroditus back to Philippi after his recovery. Fortunately Epaphroditus was able to hand the gifts of the Philippians over to Paul; see Phil. 4.18.

In Phil. 4.2 Paul addresses two women: Euodia and Syntyche. These women had helped Paul with his work earlier on, but in one way or another tensions had arisen. They belong to the young congregation as well and are encouraged to be 'of the same mind'. Another person is addressed in Phil. 4.3. He is mentioned as 'a companion'. He is asked to help both of these women in their difficult situation. Unfortunately we cannot determine with certainty the identity of this person. All we can say about him is that he must be someone who collaborated with Paul and had great authority in Philippi. Apart from the two women and the unknown companion, a certain Clement is mentioned. It says in Phil. 4.3 that he collaborated with Paul as well. He is the only one with a Latin name. This is not really surprising because, initially, Greek-speaking people in particular joined the Christian congregation, and the Romans made up only a very small part of the Christian congregation in Philippi. The Greek names for the offices in the church of the first centuries also suggest that in Philippi and elsewhere Greek-speaking people named the various offices 'episkopos' and 'diakonos' – both Greek words. There were presumably no Thracians yet in the congregation.

All in all we can list 11 people who had chosen to go the way indicated by Paul: Lydia, the goaler, two bishops, two deacons, Epaphroditus, Euodia, Syntyche, the 'companion' and Clement. We know only the professions of Lydia and the goaler. These 11 individuals probably lived in Philippi itself. Paul himself stayed in the town as well. Consequently his audience and the subsequent congregation were probably made up specifically of townspeople. People from the country visited the town only now and then, and were probably under-represented in the congregation. The people of the Christian congregation presumably belonged to the working classes, and were not very wealthy. Lydia apparently had a spacious house at her disposal (see Acts 16.15), but in 2 Cor. 8.1-3 Paul himself mentions the poverty of the congregations in Macedonia. The Philippians occasionally sent Paul financial support, but he still needed to work for a living; see 1 Thess. 2.9. Paul even mentions that they shared with him 'in the matter of giving and receiving' from the very beginning; see Phil. 4.15. This aid must have consisted of small contributions that he received from them.

The 11 people mentioned above will have belonged to different families. The average family may have consisted of two parents, two children and two slaves. Let us say that if half of these people comprised the congregation, there were 11 × 3 = 33 members of the congregation. These people were 'all the saints' addressed in this epistle around the year 60. Of course this number is very hypothetical and there are many uncertainties, but on the basis of the available data this size of the Christian congregation in Philippi is defendable.

Life was not easy for this small minority group. In Phil. 3 Paul writes about opponents who endanger the survival of the community. He uses the words 'circumcision' and 'miscircumcision', words that cannot be recognized in the English translation. The two Greek words that are rather similar have been translated as 'mutilation of the flesh' and 'circumcision'. These words make it clear that Paul points to people who propagate circumcision in line with the Jewish tradition. Paul dismisses in Phil. 3.5-7 that circumcision and other perceived privileges can still play a positive role. According to Paul, from this time onward those who believe in Christ are the true circumcised people, and those who hold on to the old rituals are mutilated people. The most important aim now is to gain Christ (Phil. 3.8) and to attain the resurrection from the dead (Phil. 3.11). It may be deduced from Acts 16.40 that a small group of believers had formed around Lydia. However, as it is certain that not all Jews had followed Paul's message, tensions were bound to arise. The appeal to follow Paul in Phil. 3.16-17 may have had to do with the fact that circumcision would mark gentile Christians as Jews. This would make them members of a permitted religion and that would have made their situation much easier. But Paul wanted to prevent this at all cost, as it would deprive the Gospel of its essence.

In this epistle Paul also discusses suffering. Suffering was connected with his own imprisonment; see Phil. 1.17; 4.14. The congregation was subjected to suffering as well; see Phil 1.29. The suffering of Christ is mentioned in Phil. 2.6-11, for example. Paul seems to discuss his own suffering and the suffering of Christ so extensively in order to encourage the Philippians in their difficult situation. The call for humility in Phil. 2.3 should certainly be read against the background of suffering. A little later, in Phil. 2.5, Paul asks the Philippians to let the same mind be in them that was in Christ Jesus. The hymn that follows shows the nature of Christ's attitude in suffering. He had humbled himself and accepted his death, even death on the cross. Paul wanted to make clear to the Philippians that they had to endure suffering in the same manner. With respect to this suffering we do not need to think of severe persecutions; there were no persecutions as yet. These emerged later in the Roman Empire, and they seldom occurred on a large scale. The suffering referred to by Paul involves the difficulties that a small minority group may face in a hostile environment. Contacts may have been terminated, their trade may have been boycotted or their jobs lost. It is easy to imagine that pressure was exerted on people to prevent them from holding on to the new belief. The inhabitants of any city were supposed to adopt the common habits and rituals and, as ever, people who were out of line were barely tolerated. Not only was the religion of the Christians not allowed, but it forbade them from participating in the cult of the Emperor. Everywhere in Philippi Christians were reminded of the fact that other religions played first fiddle and that the Christian belief was not accepted. Paul summons the Philippians to hold on to their joy in life in spite of such difficulties. The words 'joy', 'rejoice' and other words from the same root are often found in this epistle; see, for example, Phil. 1.25; 2.17-18; 3.1; 4.4. With such statements Paul wants to encourage the congregation to cheerfully persist in spite of the opposition and suffering they endure.

On the basis of the assumption that the congregation of Philippi consisted of about 33 people in the initial period, we can look ahead to the following centuries. It is generally accepted that at the beginning of the fourth century 10 per cent of the population of the Roman Empire had joined the Christian Church. The need for rooms of their own to meet became stronger as the number of Christians increased. In the middle of the fourth century about 50 per cent of the population were Christians and by that time they had taken over the government in the Roman Empire. For Philippi this would mean that there were about 1,000 Christians in Philippi shortly after the year 300, and even 5,000 around the year 350. The American scholar Rodney Stark conducted copious research into the growth processes of religious movements. Partly on the basis of his findings I would like to propose that the number of Christians in Philippi grew by about 15 per cent per decade, resulting in the following rounded figures:

- 33 members in the year 60
- 58 members in the year 100

- 233 members in the year 200
- 945 members in the year 300

Obviously there are many uncertainties here. The growth of the church was definitely not as regular as these figures suggest. The departure of just one family would have meant a real loss at the end of the first century. On the other hand, the congregation would have increased enormously if Christians from other parts of the Empire had settled in Philippi. Be this as it may, such hypothetical numbers are defendable. We will see later on that additional available information does not conflict with these numbers.

3

The Epistle to the Philippians and Roman Philippi

The outline of first-century Philippi, and especially of its Christian congregation, gives us a better understanding of the Epistle to the Philippians because we know about the background of the addressees. We should take this background into account when reading the Epistle. It is not a part of a tradition that is written in stone and is only helpful to formulate Christian belief or to found dogmas upon, but it is an epistle written to people of flesh and blood. These people tried to earn a living, to hold out amidst fellow citizens who did not care for this new belief. We should try to understand this epistle then as a first-century document written specifically to these Philippians. In general we should always interpret ancient texts as writings produced during a certain period, in specific circumstances and intended for a particular group of people. Only then may the question be asked if such documents are still useful for people of the twenty-first century. Biblical texts are sometimes appropriated by people in order to fulfil their needs or to confirm their creed. A clear example will serve to illustrate what I mean. The very well-known words of Ps. 23.1, 'The Lord is my shepherd', are often interpreted to mean that the Lord is the shepherd of the reader of this text. However, in this Psalm the author of these words states that the Lord is *his* shepherd and that He will be his shepherd even under the most difficult circumstances.

Clearly, I do not want to prevent people from appropriating these words and considering them useful in their situation, but for a correct exegesis we should be aware of the original background of such ancient texts.

These remarks apply to the Pauline epistles as well. They were addressed to specific groups of people. The Epistle to the Philippians was specifically meant for the small Christian congregation in Macedonia who lived in the Romanized town of Philippi. This is clear not only from the prescript where the addressees are mentioned by name, but also from the fact that it refers to people who lived in Philippi, such as Epaphroditus and Syntyche, and that Paul seems to adjust to the particular Roman atmosphere of this town, which was very much felt, particularly in the city centre. Of course various cults were present in Philippi, but there was barely any room for other religions in or close to the forum. The small group of Christians had to swim against the tide.

The vocabulary which Paul uses shows in particular that he was aware of the Roman character of Philippi. He wrote this epistle in Greek but he tried to fit in with this Roman atmosphere through his choice of words. For example, in this epistle he often uses words that refer to situations in which people compete for victory. The noun 'gain' is used in Phil. 1.21; the plural occurs in Phil. 3.7. In the New Testament this word is used only once more: in Tit. 1.11. The words 'to strive side by side' in Phil. 1.27 and 'struggle beside' in Phil. 4.3 are translations of one and the same Greek verb. This verb is only used in these two verses in the New Testament. The words 'opponents' and 'to be opposed to' may be found in the Pauline epistles in Phil. 1.28; 1 Cor. 16.9; Gal. 5.17, and in five other verses in the New Testament. The word 'fellow soldier' is used only in Phil. 2.25 and in Phlm. 2 in the entire New Testament. The verb 'to strain (Forward)' is used in the New Testament only in Phil. 3.13. In addition, the noun 'goal' may be found only in this epistle, in 3.14. The word 'prize' is used by Paul in Phil. 3.14. The only other text in the New Testament where it may be found is 1 Cor. 9.24.

Such words are often used in the military jargon and in the academies for martial arts, where people were fighting for first prize. This wording was very fitting, because many matches were held in Romanized towns such as Philippi. We have seen that officials were appointed whose sole function was to organize matches. War had been a way of life for the veterans. Shortly before this epistle was written the Romans had gained the ultimate victory over the Thracians after many years of minor skirmishes. I am convinced that Paul chose these words intentionally to better communicate his message. In this way he adapted to the Philippians' social environment.

Another striking term is 'live your life' in a manner worthy of the Gospel of Christ in Phil. 1.27. The Greek verb is found only here in the Pauline epistles. Elsewhere in the New Testament it is used only in Acts 23.1. Literally it means 'to be a citizen' or 'to behave as a citizen'. The cognate noun 'citizenship' is used in the New Testament only in Phil. 3.20. Paul used these not particularly common words deliberately, as they were suited to the social environment of Philippi. Many Romans in Philippi were proud of their Roman citizenship and of the fact that they belonged to the tribus Voltinia. It is clear that they looked down on people who did not have Roman citizenship and who therefore had to do without all sorts of privileges.

Paul mentions the *praetorians*, the imperial guard, only in Phil. 1.13, in the Greek text. It is clear that they must be situated in the city where Paul was imprisoned, namely Rome. The people of Philippi were of course very well acquainted with this word, because a cohort of praetorians had been quartered there in 30 BCE by order of Octavian. It is sometimes argued that the word *praetorium* in this verse would refer to a governor's palace, with reference to governors' residences in Caesarea or in Ephesus. It is clear that this noun can mean 'governor's palace'; see, for example, Mark 15.16. However, as far as I know, in imperial times this word was only used for a governor's palace in an imperial province such as Syria. Ephesus was situated in a senatorial province, so its governor's palace cannot be meant here. The governor's palace in Caesarea would thus be the only other option. But did Paul write this epistle from Caesarea? And who were 'everyone else' in Phil. 1.13? We can imagine that Paul said with rhetorical exaggeration 'the imperial guard and everyone else', which fits the situation in Rome. However, a phrase like 'the governor's palace and everyone else' seems a little strange.

Another phrase in this context that does occur in this epistle is the people 'of the emperor's household' (Phil. 4.22). They must have lived in Rome as well. These words refer to the large circle of people who were in the service of the Emperor. It is quite conceivable that there were connections between these people and Philippi, a town where the influence of Rome was tangible. Perhaps Lydia had contacts in Rome because of her trade in purple. A rhetorical aspect may have played a part as well. It must have suited Paul that he could mention the *praetorians* in his epistle to the congregation of the 'Roman' Philippi. Besides this he could make it clear that he had contacts with people 'of the Emperor's household'.

Another striking element in this epistle is the frequent occurrence of the words 'joy' and 'to rejoice'. The noun 'joy' has been used in Phil. 1.4; 1.25; 2.2; 2.29; 4.1, the verb 'to rejoice' in Phil. 1.18 (twice); 2.17; 2.18; 2.28; 3.1; 4.4 (twice) and 4.10. In 2.17; 2.18 a compound verb is used as well (NRSV: to rejoice with). Consequently these words are used 16 times in this short epistle.

By comparison, in the much longer Epistle to the Romans the words 'joy' and 'to rejoice' are used three and four times, respectively, i.e. seven times altogether. This epistle comprises more than 7,000 words, whereas the epistle to the Philippians comprises barely more than 1,600 words! It is clear that Paul must have had a specific aim when he used these words frequently. The fact that he himself was in prison – evidently an awful situation – may have played a role. He knew that it is very difficult to hold on to joy in life when all things are taken away. This may be the reason why he stresses in this epistle time and again that the Philippians should rejoice.

It should be noted here that Paul barely reacted against the culture that prevailed in Philippi. He did not incite the population to resist, and did not ask them to abolish their deities, but he did urge them to concentrate specifically on Jesus Christ and to follow him in spite of the ensuing difficulties. He asked them to hold on to their joy in their suffering and to continue to do well in a hostile environment. However, it is very clear that especially Phil. 2.6-11, the Christ Hymn, left little room for whomever or whatever beside the Lord. The readers and listeners must have understood that veneration of the Emperor or other dignitaries was impossible for people who would honestly confess that 'Jesus Christ is Lord' (Phil. 2.11). The word 'Lord' can have a very general meaning, but this verse makes it clear that according to Paul, Jesus Christ is superior to all 'Lords', i.e. all rulers in this world.

In this respect Phil. 3.20 should be mentioned as well. Paul stated there that we are expecting from heaven 'a Saviour, the Lord Jesus Christ'. It is the Greek word *soter* that has been translated as 'Saviour' here. The word *soter* had been used to describe kings and for other rulers for a long time. Roman emperors were called *soter* as well. Paul proclaimed that Jesus Christ is the 'Soter'. The believers' citizenship is in heaven and it is from there that Jesus Christ will come as 'Soter'. The Romans in Philippi belonged to the tribus Voltinia; their citizenship was in Rome and the emperor was officially their 'Soter'. It is true that the Emperor is not mentioned in Paul's statements, but it is also evident that according to him only one has the real power: Jesus Christ, the Lord, the Saviour.

It becomes clear from this epistle, as from the other Paulines, that Paul had received some rhetorical schooling. He wrote his epistles in accordance with the authorial standards, though he put his own stamp on them. I consider this epistle as one coherent document. I am aware of the various theories regarding two or more epistles that would have been combined into one epistle. However, up until now no unanimity has been reached regarding the extent of these letters, nor who did it, and why and when. In any case such an intervention must have taken place very early on, because no trace has been found in the manuscripts. As long as no evidence is given for such a partition theory, I will interpret this epistle just as it is handed down to us: as one coherent epistle.

With the help of handbooks in classical rhetoric we may outline this epistle as follows:

- Phil. 1.1-2, the *prescript*, containing the names of the senders and the addressees and with a salutation.
- Phil. 1.3-26, the *exordium* (introduction), in which the author thanks God for knowing these faithful people and in which he mentions his own situation which he is able to manage.
- Phil. 1.27-30, the *propositio* (proposition), in which Paul mentions the main issue: live your life in a manner worthy of the Gospel of Christ.
- Phil. 2.1–3.21, the *probatio* (argumentation), where the thesis of the proposition is founded thoroughly.

- Phil. 4.1-20, the *peroratio* (conclusion), which repeats some important arguments, mentions certain aspects that need to be corrected, and eventually reminds the Philippians of the gifts Epaphroditus brought to Paul on behalf of the Philippians.
- Phil. 4.21-23, the *postscript*, with a farewell and a blessing.

3.1 Philippians 1

The wording of the prescript in Phil. 1.1-2 is similar to the prescripts of other Pauline epistles, but here Timothy is mentioned next to Paul. Rom. 1.1 speaks of Paul alone, whereas in 1 Thess. 1.1 there are three senders: Paul, Silvanus and Timothy. It seems probable that the contribution of Timothy and others is quite small, both here and in the other epistles. The others who are mentioned in the prescripts must have agreed with the contents of these epistles. The way the author speaks about Timothy in Phil. 2.19 confirms that Timothy was not really the co-author of this epistle. Moreover, throughout this epistle the first-person singular has been used for the verbal forms, which also points to one author: Paul. Paul and Timothy are called 'servants of Christ Jesus'. In Rom. 1.1 Paul mentions himself as a servant and as an apostle. In 1 Cor. 1.1; 2 Cor. 1.1; Gal. 1.1 Paul calls himself an apostle. We will see that the title 'apostle' is used in the epistle to the Philippians as well, in 2.25, but here it refers strikingly to Epaphroditus.

The addressees are the 'saints', the members of the congregation in Philippi, 'in Christ Jesus'. The prepositional formulas 'in Christ', 'in God' and similar formulas are used very often by Paul. With this type of formula he means to say that Christ or God are closely associated with 'the saints' in Philippi. One might say that depending on the exact formula Christ or God defines the saints more closely. In 1 Cor. 1.2, for example, the same word 'saints' has been used for the addressees.

It should be noted here that Paul mentions 'bishops and deacons'. These words point to a later time in Paul's missionary period, the time when there was apparently some sort of organization. These offices cannot yet be described precisely, but the bishop must have been an overseer, whereas the deacon would have had the task of giving assistance in the community. Of course these offices did not yet have the specific roles they received in later times, but the first traces of a later development may be distinguished here. It is evident from the manner in which they are mentioned that these officials already had a certain status in the congregation of Philippi. Phil. 1.3-26 may be considered the *exordium* (introduction), in which Paul makes the Philippians receptive for his message on the basis of their common memories. He thanks God in the first passage (Phil. 1.3-11) for the Philippians, for their sharing in the Gospel and for their love. It was usual in ancient epistles to start with words of thanks. We can see this passage as a *captatio benevolentiae*, benevolent words in order to appeal to the goodwill of the addressees. The phrasing is rather exuberant. The words 'all', 'every' and 'constantly' in the NRSV are all derived from the same Greek word. In all the other Pauline epistles, with the exception of the Epistle to the Galatians, we find a thanksgiving as well. In this manner the author won the addressees over. After these friendly words it was easier to mention negative points where necessary. Paul praises the Philippians for the belief they showed from the first day on. It is clear from these verses that there is a cordial relationship between Paul and the Philippians. The fact that Paul is in prison is not harmful to their relationship; see verse 7. Paul expresses the ardent wish to see them very soon and he prays (verse 9) that they will grow in their love in order to be blameless on the Day of Christ. The contents of this paragraph may be paraphrased as: you are doing very well and should continue in this manner.

Other subjects are discussed in the following paragraph, verses 12–26. Paul addresses the Philippians using the Greek word for 'brothers'. In the NRSV this is translated as 'beloved' and in 3.13; 4.8. In 4.21 the same Greek word has been translated as 'friends'. Elsewhere this word has been translated as 'brothers and sisters'; see 1.14; 3.1; 3.17; 4.1. It is clear that Paul uses the common phrase of his time; of course he did not mean to exclude the 'sisters' with this word.

Paul speaks about his own situation first. He is in prison, but, apparently in contrast to what people may have expected, this situation has 'helped to spread the gospel'. Paul probably refers to the fact that he has the opportunity now to preach the gospel in places where he had not yet been. Possibly it is also suggested here that the way in which he is enduring this awful situation has commanded respect and that therefore his preaching has attracted attention. In this way Paul's being in prison has 'helped to spread the gospel'.

The entire imperial guard and everyone else sees what is happening. I have already discussed the word *praetorium*, imperial guard. In my opinion Paul intends to state that the praetorians in Rome and many more people from the circle around them know now that his imprisonment is because of his choice of a life in Christ. The reference to the *praetorium* must have been understandable for the Philippians because the praetorians had been quartered in Philippi since the battle of Actium in 31 BCE. With such a reference Paul clearly fits in with the Philippian situation.

Another effect of Paul's imprisonment is that the brothers dared to speak the word with greater boldness (verse 14). People may have expected that the preaching of the gospel would be endangered by Paul's imprisonment, but the opposite is the case. The manner in which Paul endures his imprisonment encourages the brothers and sisters in such a way that they are doing more for the Gospel. Nevertheless, it appears that there are some darker aspects. Several people preach the Gospel, but some have dishonourable motives (verse 15). To whom does Paul refer here? And can it be true that such behaviour does not bother him? He says that the most important point for him is the fact that the Gospel will be preached (verse 18), and it is apparently even more important than the fact that some people have dishonourable motives. Paul refers to them in verse 17, where he states that these people intend 'to increase my suffering in my imprisonment'. Of course this reminds us of the harsh words in Phil. 3.2. Is Paul speaking there about the same people he refers to in 1.15-17? I do not think so. We do not find the fierceness and the anger of Phil. 3.2 in these verses. Moreover, these preachers seem to live in the area where Paul is imprisoned, and thus probably in the neighbourhood of Rome (see verses 14 and 17), whereas the warnings in Chapter 3 concern preachers with whom the Philippians are confronted. The statements in 1.15-17 may be related to self-interest, to envy because of Paul's success and perhaps to a struggle for power. However, in spite of these darker aspects Paul rejoices in the preaching of the Gospel.

Paul will continue to rejoice because he is sure that his situation will end in his deliverance owing to the prayer of the Philippians and the help of the Spirit of Jesus Christ. The word 'deliverance' can refer to release from prison, but also to eschatological salvation. None of these notions may be excluded here. In the first case deliverance means that Paul can fulfil his task to preach the Gospel following his deliverance. In the second case Paul may have wanted to refer to the moment he comes before God when he can defend himself; cf. the use of similar words in Job 13.16 (LXX). The interpretation in an eschatological sense may be the more probable. In the following verses it becomes clear that Paul is not certain that he will be released from prison, but he is certain that Christ will be exalted in his body, 'whether by life or by death' (verse 20). Whatever will happen, it means a release for Paul. Although he esteems life greatly, to him life is Christ, and dying is gain; see verse 21. I have made clear that words such as 'gain' fit very well with the Roman situation of Philippi, where games and matches were the order of the day. Paul can even say that *dying* is gain for him, but he does not yet know what will happen, though he is sure that he will continue to preach about Christ. Paul considers the two possibilities: to depart and be with Christ, or to remain in the flesh. He cannot decide, but finishes these sentences in verse 25 with the conclusion that he will remain and stay with the Philippians to further their progress and joy in faith. This conclusion seems to contradict the last words of verse 20, 'by life or by death', when he did not yet know what would happen. The conclusion in verses 25–6 should be interpreted as an emotional exclamation, founded more on Paul's ardent wish than on certain knowledge.

In the final verses of this chapter, the *propositio*, the main thesis of this epistle is formulated. Paul summons the Philippians 'to live' according to the gospel of Jesus Christ. This appeal is itself not surprising, but the wording is very special. The verb used by Paul literally means 'to be a citizen', 'to exercise citizenship'. Paul must have chosen this word carefully, like the noun 'citizenship' in 3.20. In my opinion he wants to join in with the specific political Roman situation of Philippi, where many inhabitants were proud of their Roman citizenship. Paul usually uses another Greek verb for 'to live', or 'to walk', in the meaning of moral conduct, as in Phil. 3.17; 3.18. In these verses this word is used with both positive and negative connotations, respectively, but in 1.27 he uses 'to be a citizen' for the manner in which the Philippians should behave. The only reason I can think of for Paul's use in 1.27 and 3.20 of such unusual words is that he wants to adapt as far as possible to the Roman vocabulary which was prevalent in Philippi.

Paul urges the Philippians to live as citizens according to the rules which belong to their citizenship. In this particular case he is referring to the citizenship of heaven; cf. 3.20. Citizens who have a citizenship in heaven should live according to the Gospel of Christ. In my opinion, in this verse and in 3.20, Paul contrasts the very desirable Roman citizenship with the citizenship that is connected with heaven.

An important aspect of this life as a good citizen is unity in the Philippian congregation. Paul asks the Philippians to stand firm 'in one spirit', 'with one mind'. In this epistle he discusses unity in the church several times; see, for example, Phil. 2.2; 4.2. We may guess that he has heard about some dissension. Paul wants the Philippians to be of one mind.

The phrase 'to strive side by side' reminds us again of the specific Roman situation where all sorts of games were played very often and where the competing teams tried to win first prize through their joint efforts. Paul wants the addressees to work together for the faith of the Gospel. They should not be afraid of their opponents. Paul states in verse 28 that the opponents will be destroyed whereas the faithful people will be saved by God. It is not clear who these opponents are. In 1.15-17 people were mentioned who wanted to increase his suffering, and in 3.2-4 Paul speaks about people who preach a message that differs from his own. In 3.18-19 enemies of the cross are mentioned. Perhaps we should not differentiate between these groups. It is very possible that these groups – or some of them – overlapped. In any case, Paul speaks here of opponents who could intimidate the addressees. The members of the young Christian congregation were not accepted in society because they chose not to live the Roman life. Paul considers this discord to be evidence of the opponents' ruin and of the faithful's salvation. In this verse the meaning of 'salvation' must certainly be eschatological; see verse 19 as well. Paul wants to comfort the believing community whose members live in difficult circumstances, but who will share in future salvation.

In verse 29 Paul argues that believing in Christ is a privilege granted by God, but suffering for Christ is also a privilege. These words are clearly meant to encourage the Christians in Philippi. They form a minority group, and as such they are vulnerable to all sorts of opposition. According to Paul they should not be afraid of such opposition: it is part of the life of Christians. What is more, it is a privilege granted by God. They saw earlier what happened with Paul himself and now they hear that he is undergoing the same struggle again. In verse 20 it was argued that Paul's situation could end in his death. Nevertheless, the Philippians should react to their difficult circumstances in a positive way. Again the word 'struggle' in verse 30 is a word derived from the jargon that was used in the theatre for gladiatorial combat and for other games.

3.2 Philippians 2

In the *probatio*, Chapters 2 and 3, the main thesis (1.27-30) is founded on several arguments and illustrated with examples. The strongest argument is undoubtedly the urge in 2.5-11 to live as Jesus Christ lived. Besides this argument several other subjects are mentioned, such as his sending of Timothy and Epaphroditus to Philippi.

The rhetorical statements in verse 1 mean of course that there is 'encouragement in Christ', 'consolation from love', 'sharing in the Spirit', and 'compassion and sympathy'. Therefore Paul asks them to make his joy complete through their unanimity. With diverse phrasing Paul stresses that their sense of unity must be mutual. Selfish ambition and conceit may not be found in the congregation, but they should respect each other; even more, they should with humility regard others as better than themselves, and they should all look to the interests of others. The stress on unity is striking. As has been said earlier, such statements give the impression that Paul had reason to write about unity several times in this epistle, in spite of the fact that he is generally full of praise for the Philippian congregation.

Verse 5 is the introduction of what is usually called the Christ Hymn. Paul asks the Philippians to imitate the attitude or mind of Christ. In verses 6–11 this attitude is described with words that are undoubtedly derived from a hymn. The vocabulary and the line of thought lead most scholars to assume that this hymn existed already, though it is possible, of course, that Paul himself composed these verses. However, the way in which this hymn is connected with the preceding verse by a relative pronoun – 'who' – confirms the assumption that Paul inserted this hymn into his epistle. This hymn consists of two parts: 2.6-8 and 2.9-11. The first part speaks about Christ's humiliation; the second part about his exaltation. Christ himself is the acting person in the first part; in the second part it is God who takes action.

It is stated in verses 6–7 that Christ was in the form of God, but he was prepared to abandon this high position and to become like a slave, born in human likeness. The relation between Christ and God is considered very close here, but Christ and God are not equated to each other. It is not said that Christ is God. Paul would have found it impossible to make such a statement since, being a Jew, he must have stressed that there was only one God. Neither is Christ equated to a human being. The difference between Christ and God is maintained, as is the difference between Christ and human beings. The relevant phrases in these verses are: 'in the form of God', 'equality with God', 'taking the form of a slave', 'in human likeness' and 'in human form'. The last word is the translation of a different Greek word than the word 'form' in the first and the third phrase, but it is very difficult to represent these small nuances in a translation.

This part of the hymn has its climax in verse 8 where it says that Christ had been obedient even to the death on the cross. With these last words Paul states explicitly that Christ did what is almost humanly impossible.

The contrast with the second part of this hymn is striking. Christ suffered the most profound humiliation according to verses 6–8, but in the second part, verses 9–11, it is shown that God highly exalted him. How God exalted Christ is explained in the following sentences. God has granted him the highest name that exists and therefore all people will kneel before him and everyone will confess that Jesus Christ is the Lord. Literally it is said that every soul in heaven and on earth and under the earth will kneel before him. Therefore no creature will be excluded from kneeling before Christ and from confessing that he is the Lord. We know the Greek word for 'Lord', *kurios*, from the liturgical formula *kyrie eleison*: Lord have mercy. This word *kurios* was used for God in the Greek translation of the Old Testament, the so-called Septuagint. In the New Testament it is frequently used for Jesus Christ, but it is also used regularly for any man. The wording here shows clearly that it is meant as a high title: 'Jesus Christ is Lord.' The Philippians would complete this confession with the words: 'And nobody else.' It should be repeated here that the Roman Emperor was honoured as *kurios*, or in Latin as *dominus*, and he was mentioned as *divus Augustus*, divine Augustus, on coins and in inscriptions and so on. The confession that Jesus Christ is the Lord makes it clear that Christians did not agree with the required reverence for the Emperor of Rome. Especially in Roman Philippi the statement that Jesus Christ is the Lord was not without risk.

The final words of verse 11 give all honour to God. The confession that Jesus Christ is the Lord does not diminish God Himself. On the contrary, God is honoured by the fact that all creatures will kneel before Jesus Christ and that they will confess that Jesus Christ is the Lord. Actually this hymn closes in verse 11 with a twofold eulogy: one with respect to Jesus Christ and one with respect to God.

In the next paragraph (2.12-18), Paul reminds the beloved faithful people in Philippi to obey him as they have always obeyed him, and to work out their own salvation. The noun 'salvation' here refers to an eschatological salvation. This noun can have the meaning 'deliverance' or 'welfare' as well; cf. 1.19-28. It means 'being delivered' and also its result, the state of salvation. It is clear that Paul reminds the Philippians of their former attitude towards his preaching. They obeyed his message in the past, and they should therefore obey him now more than ever, since he cannot now visit them. They should not forget what happened earlier.

There is a certain contradiction between the words of verse 12 and the statement in verse 13. In verse 12 Paul says that the addressees should work out their own salvation, and in verse 13 he says that it is God who enables them 'to will and to work for his good pleasure'. But the phrase in verse 13 does not diminish the urgent appeal to the congregation in verse 12. On the contrary, the works of the congregation in Philippi will be strengthened by the works of God; cf. 1.6: 'God who began a good work among you will bring it to completion by the day of Jesus Christ.'

The following verses affirm the appeal that was expressed in verse 12. The members of the Christian congregation should do all things 'without murmuring'. It is very possible that the word 'murmuring' is derived from the Septuagint. It is used there, for example, in Ex. 16.7-8, and refers to the complaints of the Israelites against God. Paul does not use this noun anywhere else in his epistles, a fact that may confirm that he is alluding to an older tradition. The ultimate goal is that the Philippians will be blameless and innocent 'in the midst of a crooked and perverse generation'. In this way Paul can be proud of them on the Day of Christ and his efforts will not have been in vain. It is certain that Paul alludes to the Septuagint in verse 15: the exact phrase 'a crooked and perverse generation' is found in Deut. 32.5 (LXX). The NRSV gives these words of Deut. 32.5 in the reverse order, 'perverse and crooked', probably on the basis of the Hebrew text of Deut. 32.5. Paul does not say that the Philippians belong to such a crooked generation, but he warns them to live honestly so that they will never belong to such people.

It is striking to read in verse 17 that Paul refers again to the possibility that he will be sentenced to death; see 1.20. He uses words that are known from the cult of Dionysus, for example. Wine would be poured out as a libation and it is even said that Dionysus himself was poured out. This cultic term points to bloodshed here, as in some other texts. Paul takes into account the possibility that he may die shortly and he considers his death as an offering that is added to the offering of the Philippians' faith, which is regarded by Paul as an offering to God as well.

In the final words of verse 17 and in verse 18 Paul declares that he himself will rejoice and he will rejoice together with the Philippians. He writes these words in spite of the apparently threatening and unsafe situation in which he finds himself. These words are undoubtedly meant to encourage the congregation in Philippi, which has its own problems as a minority group in a thoroughly Romanized town. This is also the reason why he concludes this passage with the order that they should also hold on to their joy.

Paul is trying to encourage the Philippian Christians in another way in the next paragraph, in verses 19–23. He will send Timothy as soon as possible. The Philippians know Timothy very well and he will be concerned for their welfare. All others are seeking their own interests; cf. 1.15-17. This statement can only be interpreted as rhetorical exaggeration. Many more people helped Paul in preaching the Gospel. In the next passage Epaphroditus is mentioned as a co-worker, and a fellow soldier and other co-workers are mentioned in 4.3. Of course it was not Paul's intention to disqualify all of these colleagues. He only wants to stress Timothy's exceptional talents. Paul's goal is that he himself will be cheered by news about the addressees and that they will be supported by Timothy.

Timothy was mentioned as one of the senders in 1.1, but it is clear from these verses that he is not the real sender. He must of course have agreed with the contents of this epistle but Paul himself is clearly the leading man. The name 'Timothy' literally means 'one who honours god'. It had been a well-known name for several centuries, and consequently it is not a particularly Christian name. Timothy was one of Paul's helpers and according to the Book of Acts he joined Paul on several journeys. Paul says he hopes to send him shortly and finishes these sentences with the words that he hopes to be able to visit them himself very soon.

The unremitting suspense about the uncertain future is evident. In 1.20 Paul shows that he may die soon; in 1.25 he states that he 'will remain'; in 2.17 he believes again that he may be sentenced to death, and here in 2.23 he repeats his hope that he will be able to visit Philippi again. In the final passage of chapter 2 Paul says that he considers it necessary to send Epaphroditus, the Apostle of the Philippians, to Philippi. In the NRSV this word has been translated as 'messenger' in Phil. 2.25; it explains in the footnote that the Greek text has 'apostle'. In 1 Cor. 1.1; 2 Cor. 1.1, Paul uses the word 'apostle' with respect to himself, whereas the co-authors, Sosthenes in 1 Cor. 1.1 and Timothy in 2 Cor. 1.1, are called 'brother'. It is clear from these texts that Paul considers the word 'apostle' as indicating a higher status than 'brother'. The expression in these epistles makes it all the more striking that Paul uses the word 'apostle' in the Epistle to the Philippians only for Epaphroditus, the Apostle of the Philippians. There is of course a difference even in the use of 'apostle', since Paul mentions himself as 'apostle of Christ Jesus' and Epaphroditus as 'apostle of you', i.e. of the Philippians. Nevertheless the use of the word 'apostle' is striking. Could it be that he consciously calls Epaphroditus 'apostle' of the Philippians in order to shield him from any blame? Apparently Epaphroditus had not been totally successful regarding his mission; see below.

We do not know anything about Epaphroditus other than what is mentioned here and in 4.18. The name is clearly Greek in origin, referring to the goddess Aphrodite. More persons with this name are known from ancient history. In a village quite close to Philippi an inscription in Latin has been found with the name Epaphroditus, and in Philippi itself an inscription has been found with the shortened form Epaphra, also in Latin. This inscription still lies in the narthex of Basilica B. We may deduct from these verses that the Philippians had sent Epaphroditus in order to help Paul in his difficult situation, but obviously something had gone wrong: Epaphroditus had become seriously ill. The Philippians had heard about his illness, and the fact that they had heard about it distressed Epaphroditus. After his recovery he intended to go back to Philippi to put their minds at rest. These messages must have travelled from and to Philippi, which must have taken time. For this reason it is sometimes argued that Rome cannot have been the place where Paul wrote this epistle while he was in prison. However, I do not see any objection to the presumption that Epaphroditus stayed in Rome for two months or so. Following his recovery he could return to Philippi, and it is very understandable that he would really have liked to go back.

We get the impression from these verses that Paul thought it possible that the Philippians might blame Epaphroditus for the partial lack of success of his assignment. They may have believed that Epaphroditus' illness had burdened Paul, whereas they had intended to support him. We do not know for sure, but in any case we know from these verses that Epaphroditus had fallen sick and we know that Paul thinks it necessary to make a plea in favour of Epaphroditus. He asks the Philippians insistently to welcome him in the Lord and to honour him, because he had done a good job and he had come close to death for the work of Christ. It is probable that Epaphroditus himself brought this epistle with him when he returned to Philippi.

At the end of this epistle Paul stresses again that he received the generous gifts they sent by Epaphroditus; see also 4.18. It is clear from these passages that Paul wants the Philippians to receive Epaphroditus in a very friendly manner. Phil. 2. 25-30 and Phil. 4.18 reflect the same situation, and for this reason as well it is very unlikely that Phil. 4.18 originally belonged to another Epistle to the Philippians, as is sometimes argued.

3.3 Philippians 3

Paul begins this new section with a summons to rejoice in the Lord. We have already seen that words such as 'to rejoice' and 'joy' are frequently used in this epistle. Paul incites the Philippians several times to hold on to the joy in the Lord. After these words he refers to writing 'the same things'. The question is what does he means by 'the same things', and why does he speak so bluntly about his opponents in verse 2? Different options have been suggested. In my opinion the more probable explanation is that Paul wants to discuss the way they should 'work out their own salvation' again and again; see 2.12. He fiercely argues that many people live as enemies of the cross, but his addressees should imitate his example and expect their Saviour from heaven. The Saviour will conform their bodies to the body of his glory. This point is so essential for Paul that he does not avoid using terms of abuse. He calls people who preach a different gospel his opponents, 'dogs', 'evil workers' and 'those who mutilate the flesh'. By using such a vocabulary Paul certainly intends to make it as clear as possible that these opponents violate the Gospel he preaches.

The difference between the preceding passage and the words in 3.2 is sometimes used as an argument for a division of this epistle into two or even more epistles. However, in my opinion there is no need to reason like this. Paul was rather hot-tempered, especially when his former traditional belief was discussed; see also Gal. 2.14; 5.12. In the Epistle to the Philippians salvation is discussed in several ways, and Paul becomes enraged if somebody dares to question his statements.

A dog is an unclean animal, but in Judaism it used to refer to the gentiles as well; see, for example, Mark 7.27. The gentiles were ritually unclean. Actually Paul is arguing now that his opponents are ritually unclean because of their points of view. In the following verses he will make it clear which reprehensible ideas they preached. I do not see any reason why the noun 'dogs' (in Greek *kynes*) should be explained as an indication for the Cynic philosophers, as some authors have argued. This explanation does not make any sense here; it even interrupts the reasoning. The three indications – 'dogs', 'evil workers' and 'those who mutilate the flesh' – refer to one and the same group of opponents, and here as elsewhere it becomes clear that Paul refers to people who purport to preach the Gospel, but who actually mutilate its most essential point. They preach the Gospel in an evil manner. In Paul's opinion they garble the message of Jesus Christ.

The contrast between the last word of verse 2 (literally: mutilation) and the noun 'circumcision' in verse 3 betrays something of the message of Paul's opponents. It is translated in the NRSV as 'those who mutilate the flesh', but the word used here, *katatome* (miscircumcision), is a corruption of the Greek word *peritome* (circumcision). This makes it clear that the preaching which Paul wants to dispute must have had something to do with elements such as circumcision, law and righteousness. Paul is afraid that the message of his opponents will render his labour in vain. Therefore he is rather crude in his statements. The opponents seem to be proud of their achievements, but Paul turns things around: 'For it is we who are the circumcision.' The roles have now been reversed.

Paul continues with the remark that if they have any achievements, he himself has even more (verses 4–5). We can imagine that Paul's anger has cooled a little and that he smiled as he wrote these sentences. He had been circumcised, he was a member of the people of Israel, of the tribe of Benjamin and so on. In verse 6 Paul even mentions among his 'achievements' that he had been a persecutor of the church (cf. Gal. 1.13), and that he was blameless 'as to righteousness under the law'. Paul refers here to righteousness as it was taught by Jewish teachers on the basis of their interpretation of the law. In these sentences Paul divides his life into two periods. Verses 5–6 sum up his alleged merits, but he does not want to think like this any more. He now considers them a loss because of Christ. Subjects that were important to him have become irrelevant. He has other interests now: knowing Jesus Christ. In order to gain Christ, all things of value in his former life are now considered worthless.

Verse 9 begins with a very short phrase: 'and (that I may) be found in him', i.e. in Christ. We saw earlier that formulas such as 'in Christ' or 'in the Lord' qualify the object to which it belongs; see 1.1; 1.13; 2.1, and so on. Here in Phil. 3.9 Paul wants to express his hope that he will be connected inseparably with Christ. He then brings out the contrast between his own righteousness that comes 'from the law' with the righteousness that comes 'through faith in

Christ', the righteousness from God based on faith. There is no big difference between 'righteousness of his own that comes from the law' and the 'righteousness under the law' (verse 6). Here in verse 9 the emphasis is more on the righteousness that is purported to arise from the law. Paul considers it now to be a fallacy that righteousness could be attained on the basis of the law; on the contrary, it can only be attained through faith in Christ. The nouns 'faith' and 'righteousness' are repeated here. It does not make any sense to translate the first use of 'faith' as 'faithfulness' (of Christ), as some authors argue. The word 'faith' is used twice here and very close together. It must have the same meaning in both cases. Paul nearly trips over his own words in trying to connect faith with righteousness as closely as possible; but it remains a complex issue. In 1.27-28 there is a connection between faith and salvation. In 2.12 it is said that the addressees should work out their own salvation and in this passage in chapter 3 it is argued that righteousness will be obtained through faith and based on faith; see Gal. 2.16; 3.1-13. It is apparently impossible for Paul to find one single formula that does justice to all aspects of this subject. In chapter 2.12-16 ethical provisions were given, but see 2.13. In addition, in 3.9 the importance of faith is stressed.

The goal Paul wishes to achieve is further elaborated on in verse 10: to know Christ and the power of his resurrection, and so on. 'To know' here does not refer to scientific knowledge, but it means to be acquainted with, as, for example, in 1 Sam. 3.17. Next to it 'the power of his resurrection', 'the sharing of his sufferings' and eventually 'becoming like him in his death' are mentioned. Paul wants to experience the power of his resurrection and to share Jesus' sufferings, and even wants to be like him in his death. These elements are closely connected with each other; see Rom. 6.5. Thus he will hopefully reach the ultimate goal: the resurrection from the dead (verse 11). Of course this resurrection is not exactly the same concept as salvation or righteousness, but Paul can use these different wordings for the same goal that he always keeps in mind.

In the next passage of this chapter, verses 12–16, Paul frequently uses vocabulary that is derived from games and matches. As was said above he consciously chose such words in order to fit in with the specific situation of Philippi. He outlines life here as a match which people should try to win. He himself is still fighting. He has not yet reached the finish line, but he presses on to gain the award connected with this match. The second phrase of verse 12 is translated in the NRSV as 'have already reached the goal'. This translation is not wrong in itself, but it obscures the connection with verse 15. The second statement of verse 12 literally says: 'not that I am already perfect'. In verse 15 the adjective from the same root is used: 'those of us who are perfect' (NRSV: 'who are mature'). Thus, on the one hand, he says in verse 12 that he is not yet perfect; on the other hand, he includes himself in verse 15 in those who are. This contradiction is caused by different emphases. In verse 12 it is stressed that he is still on the path to the ultimate achievement, in verse 15 it is stated that they are already on the path that leads to this ultimate achievement; see also 1 Cor. 9.24-27. Like an athlete he strains forward to the finish line, i.e. the award of attaining the resurrection from the dead (verse 11), salvation (1.28; 2.12) or the righteousness from God based on faith (3.9). He does not want to think of his former life any more because it did not have any value; see also verse 7. For Paul the only thinkable object is the finish line, which is described in verse 14 as 'the prize of the heavenly call of God' and it is qualified with the phrase 'in Christ Jesus'. Here, as elsewhere, Paul refers to the fact that God is said to call people time and again in order for them to attain the prize promised in this call; cf. Gal. 1.15; 1 Thess. 2.12. This passage is concluded with the appeal to all to be of the same mind. Nonetheless, Paul considers the possibility that some people can have different opinions; God himself will reveal the true point of view. Paul was remarkably tolerant here, whereas in 3.2, for example, he fiercely rejected statements with which he did not agree. In 3.2-9 the way to gain Christ was discussed. This is a crucial point of Paul's message, and Paul expresses very strong views therein. Consequently the disagreements referred to in verse 15 must be minor ones. In verse 16 he asks the Philippians again to adhere to what has already been achieved.

In the final paragraph of this chapter (verses 17–21), Paul starts with the summons to imitate him and to look at people who have followed the example of Paul and his colleagues. With these words Paul is referring to people who behave in the way that Paul taught them, as in Phil. 2, for instance. Of course the contents of faith, as explained in the foregoing section, belong to the required behaviour as well. Paul's appeal to the addressees is all the more pressing, since many people live as enemies of the cross of Christ (verse 18). He says that he has spoken about these people often, but apparently to no avail. Paul's emotional interest in this subject is stressed because he repeats his words with tears in his eyes. He does not say here who these enemies are exactly, but Paul must have people in mind who had or still have some relation with the Christian congregation. He is not referring here to the gentiles. The fact that they live as enemies of the cross indicates that they know of the message of the cross as Paul preaches it, but wilfully disregard it. Some of their features are mentioned in verse 19. First, Paul says that they will be destroyed in the end. This conclusion is based on their behaviour: 'Their god is the belly, their glory is in their shame; their minds are set on earthly things.' These statements are rather general. Perhaps Paul is speaking again about people who purport to preach the Gospel but who are distorting it according to Paul. The phrase 'their god is the belly' must refer to unbridled gluttony; cf. Rom. 16.18. They are proud of their way of life, but according to Paul it is this which marks their shame. They are only concerned with earthly things, things of no value, things that will become lost. These people represent a negative model; they are not to be imitated.

Paul's thoughts run faster than his ability to express them. We might add at the end of verse 19 or at the beginning of verse 20 a phrase like: 'but our minds are set on heavenly things'. And then the sentence could be continued with 'because our citizenship is in heaven'. What Paul wants to say is clear, but his phrases are very short. The 'earthly things' in verse 19 are evidently meant to be set against 'in heaven' in verse 20: the minds of the enemies of the cross are set on earthly things, but Paul and his followers are oriented towards heaven, and their citizenship is in heaven. I have discussed the word 'citizenship' above; see also 1.27. This is the only instance where it is used in the New Testament and its use is undoubtedly caused by the Roman context of his addressees. However, their allegiance is not to Rome but to heaven.

It is from there that the faithful expect the Lord Jesus Christ as their Saviour. This statement may have been a reference to the Roman belief that they were dependent on the Emperor for their salvation. I have mentioned an inscription that lies at the forum (Figure 11); this gives thanks for *quies Augustae*, for the peace and the rest that was procured by the Emperor. The Romans interpreted the concept of 'salvation' as peace and rest here on earth, whereas Paul could use the noun 'salvation' in different contexts; see 1.19; 1.28; 2.12. The Greek noun that is translated here as 'saviour' was often used for kings and emperors. This honorary name is also found on coins and in inscriptions. Other rulers besides the Roman Emperor as well as deities could also be called 'Saviour' and 'Lord', but the manner in which Paul uses these words here must have been offensive to the Romans; see also 2.11.

This passage ends with the statement that he, the Saviour, will transform the body of our humiliation into the body of his glory. Paul uses different wordings for this radical change; cf. 1 Cor. 15.43; 15.51-53. After this transformation there will be a certain similarity between the bodies of mankind and Jesus' glorified body. The Saviour will do all this through his unlimited power. It looks as though Paul does not have enough words to emphasize the power of the Lord; cf., for example, 1 Cor. 15.27. The second part of this verse states that there are no limits to the power of Jesus Christ. It must be made clear that it is the Lord Jesus Christ who controls all power in this world, and the power of the Emperor exists only on the surface.

3.4 Philippians 4

Phil. 4.1-20 is the *peroratio*, the concluding section, in which Paul repeats some important items such as unity in the congregation, and he asks them again to be ethical and unimpeachable. The first verse of this chapter starts with a summons to stand firm, as described above. This appeal concludes the foregoing passage, and it marks the transition to the next section. It appears that Paul is trying to find as many kindly words as possible. He uses the word 'beloved' twice. Its first use has been translated in the NRSV as the phrase 'whom I love', which is not wrong of course, but it obscures the fact of Paul's double use of the same word in one sentence. Saying that he longs for them, he calls them 'my joy and my crown'. This verse is very friendly and formulated very positively. Paul tries to win the Philippians over in order to create space for some critical remarks.

In 4.2 he specifically summons two women, Euodia and Syntyche, to be of the same mind. These two women are not mentioned anywhere else. Verse 3 states that they have struggled beside Paul in the work of the Gospel. Euodia literally means 'a good journey' and Syntyche means 'good luck'. Related names are Eutychus (Acts 20.9), the lucky one, and the Latin name Fortunatus (1 Cor. 16.17), which may also be translated as 'the lucky one'. These two women should end their conflict. There must have been discord between these women or perhaps a theological dispute. It cannot be dismissed that there was a conflict between these two women on the one hand and the congregation on the other, but the wording seems to refer to discord between these women. Apparently Paul heard about it; he warns them to stop quarrelling. Paul has already brought up the unity of the congregation in various terms in this letter; see Phil. 1.27; 2.2; 3.15 and 4.2. Phil. 3 questions rather sharply how righteousness can be received, but this dispute does not seem to play a role in the dissension between Euodia and Syntyche. If so, Paul would have expressed himself more clearly, and we would moreover expect to find the same sharpness of chapter 3 in Phil. 4.2. Perhaps we should regard Paul's appeal to be 'of the same mind' in Phil. 4.2 in the light of the struggle for power that arises so easily in a young congregation which is still finding its way and needs to find out how it should be organized. It is also possible that this young congregation was confronted with opposition and that this opposition caused tensions. What could the young congregation do against opposition from fellow citizens? The members may have thought very differently about the manner in which to react to opposition, but there may be another reason for Paul's remarks, a reason we do not know.

In the following verse Paul asks his 'loyal companion' to help these women. Who is this 'loyal companion'? We do not know. Sometimes it is argued that the Greek word that is translated as 'companion' may be a proper name, but the word Paul uses is not known as a name. This companion must have worked together with Paul. The Greek word that is translated here as 'loyal' was used in 2.20 with respect to Timothy (NRSV in 2.20: genuinely). It is clear that Paul shows much appreciation for this person. Clearly, the Philippians must have known to whom these words refer and he must have been a person with influence in the Philippian congregation. The only one I can think of who meets these requirements is the author of the so-called 'we-sections' of Acts: Acts 16.10-17; 20.5-15; 21.1-18 and 27.1–28.16. But more people may qualify for this role. Whoever he is, this man is asked to support these women in their situation of discord, when before they worked together with Paul in the work of the Gospel, as did Clement and others. This Clement is the only one in the Philippian congregation who has a Latin name. This name means 'inclined to show mercy', and was already used as a name before the emergence of Christianity.

The last phrase of verse 3 states that their names are in the book of life. We know the notion of 'a book of life', for example, from Ps. 69.29. The idea is that the names of faithful people are written down in this book. As has been said above, it is possible that Paul has a list with the names of Roman citizens in mind and that he wants to remind the Philippian congregation that the names of the faithful are in the book of life, a fact that is of course much more important in his opinion.

After this admonition Paul asks the Philippians to rejoice. I have said that the words 'joy' and 'to rejoice' are used rather frequently in this epistle. Here Paul uses the imperative 'rejoice' twice. It is apparently very important for Paul to tell the Philippians that they should hold on to their joy in spite of the problems just mentioned and in spite of the difficulties they are facing as a minority group. Verse 5 has another imperative: their gentleness should be known to everyone. They should not be quarrelsome or hateful, but friendly and accommodating. Paul motivates this appeal with the theological argument that the Lord is near. Consequently they have all the more reason to live according to the Gospel that Paul preached in Philippi.

Verses 6 and 7 may be seen as an intermezzo. Their problems, their sorrows, should be made known to God. His peace will then guard their hearts; cf. Num. 6.26. The noun 'peace' reminds us of the Hebrew word *shalom*. Like the Greek word Paul uses here *shalom* means much more than the absence of war. Its meaning comes close to the meaning of the word 'salvation'.

In verses 8 and 9 ethical requirements are again listed. These requirements are rather general. They are not written especially with regard to abuses in Philippi, but they are meant as an appeal to improve their way of life. Paul uses six adjectives to describe what the Philippians should do and he summarizes these acts with two nouns: excellence and praise. Actually he says that they should do all things that are salutary and beneficial. In verse 9 Paul mentions all traditions they have learned from Paul's preaching, his teaching and his life. That is the way they should live. These two verses are concluded with a phrase that reminds us of the words of verse 7. There it said, 'The peace of God ... will guard your hearts.' Here in verse 9 Paul says, 'The God of peace will be with you.' A similar phrase may be found in Rom. 15.33; 1 Thess. 5.23. The noun 'peace' is used here to characterize God. 'Peace', which has the same meaning as the Hebrew *shalom* here and in verse 7, is one of God's characteristics.

In the next passage, verses 10–18, Paul reminds us again of the gifts brought to him by Epaphroditus. His joy is founded 'in the Lord', but the immediate cause is that the Philippians have supported him. It is clear from Paul's wording that they had wanted to help him earlier, but did not have the means. We do not know why. Did they lack a person in their congregation who was able to perform such a task? Or were their efforts impeded by the authorities? However this may be, 'at last' they have helped Paul with their gifts. Very quickly Paul continues by saying that actually his position is not so bad. In his life he has learned to be content in any situation. The word translated here as 'content' could be translated as 'self-supporting' as well. Paul intends to make it clear that he is very glad of the gifts from the Philippians, but he is not dependent on them.

Perhaps Paul does not want to bother them owing to the 'extreme poverty' of the Macedonian churches (2 Cor. 8.2) or the difficulties the Philippians had to go through to give him these gifts. He emphasizes that he is used to experiencing all sorts of troubles. Thus he reassures them that they do not need to worry about him. He is acquainted with being both well fed and hungry. The verb Paul uses here in verse 12 literally means 'to be initiated'. The noun 'mystery' has been derived from this verb. That may be the reason for the translation 'learn the secret' in the NRSV, but in this context this verb has the meaning 'be initiated in' or 'be acquainted with'. Paul knows all these difficulties, but he can endure these things through 'him who strengthens me'. It is not clear if Paul refers to Jesus or to God with these words. Because of texts such as 2 Cor. 12.9 it may be more probable that he derives the power to endure these things from Jesus.

In verse 14 Paul takes up the item of the gifts brought to him by Epaphroditus one more time. In this way the Philippians share his distress and this makes life much more bearable for him. He reminds them of the situation that existed some years ago. By then only their congregation 'shared with me in the matter of giving and receiving' (verse 15). These words have been derived from financial transactions, as if there were an account in which it was noted what was given and what was received; cf. Phlm. 18–19. The Philippians were the only congregation that had this relationship based on mutual trust. The Greek formulation for 'Philippians' is striking. Paul gives a Latin ending to the Greek name. This is the earliest use of this formulation that has been found thus far, so Paul is apparently the author who initiated the use of this word, even though it would take a long time before this name would be used more frequently. Paul probably did this in order to adapt to the Romanized town.

In verse 16 it is said that the Philippians sent help to Paul more than once when he was in Thessalonica; cf. 1 Thess. 2.9. Such statements confirm that there was a very cordial relationship between Paul and the Philippians. Further, as in verses 11–13, he seems to argue again that he does not really need these gifts. What is important to him is the profit that accumulates to their account with God. Paul seems to ignore his own needs. What counts is that the Philippians live according to the message he had proclaimed to them.

In verse 18 Paul repeats that he is thankful. He uses other words, but it is clear that he is very pleased with the gifts he received. In his opinion they form 'a sacrifice acceptable and pleasing to God'. It cannot be a coincidence that he mentions Epaphroditus again. As became clear in the discussion of Phil. 2.25-30, Epaphroditus was not undisputed. Paul tried to smooth the way for him there. And now, right at the end of his epistle he mentions Epaphroditus once more, and in a very positive sense. Epaphroditus brought the gifts that may be considered 'a sacrifice ... pleasing to God'. After this second positive judgment of Epaphroditus Paul concludes the passage, saying that God will fulfil their needs generously. Many manuscripts read an optative here, indicating a wish, apparently owing to a certain amount of embarrassment with the firm tone of this sentence, but the oldest and most important manuscripts use the future tense. Accordingly it should be maintained that Paul promises the Philippians that God will generously reward their efforts. The redundant wording at the end of verse 19, 'in glory in Christ Jesus', emphasizes that God will amply repay the help given to Paul. The phrase 'in Christ Jesus' is used several times in the Pauline epistles. It refers to the fact that Jesus Christ covers everything that is happening in the world.

Eventually a doxology is expressed, a solemn declaration that gives all honour to God. We also find doxologies elsewhere; cf. Rom. 16.27; Gal. 1.5; Phil. 1.11 and Eph. 3.21.

In the postscript Paul asks the Philippians to greet 'every saint'. The word 'saint' refers to the members of the congregation; see Phil. 1.1. The people of Paul's circle give their regards to the Philippians. Even more people, all the saints, greet the Philippians. And then it is said: 'especially those of the Emperor's household.' These last words refer to the people who are working for the Emperor. Although these words fit the situation in Rome very well, they could be used for people serving the Emperor elsewhere. This is the only reference that Paul makes to people from the Emperor's household. We may assume that Paul consciously mentions them. Many Romans lived in Philippi, and perhaps some of them were acquaintances of the 'people of the emperor's household' as well. In any case, mentioning the Emperor's household will undoubtedly have pleased those people in Philippi who were Romans or who had good relations with Romans. Even for the authorities in Philippi it may have been important to know that there were relations between this Christian congregation and people of the Emperor's household.

The Epistle concludes with the well-known benediction: 'The grace of the Lord Jesus Christ be with your spirit'; see Gal. 6.18; Phlm. 25. In these texts the singular 'spirit' is connected with the plural 'your'. We do not need to stress the use of the singular. It may be used with regard to the desired unity of the church of Philippi, but this is not at all certain. The same wording in Phlm. 25 does not refer to unity in a situation of discord! The noun 'spirit' refers to that part of the human being which is suited to communicate with God. As elsewhere, Paul looks for the presence of the Lord's grace in the spirit of the Philippians.

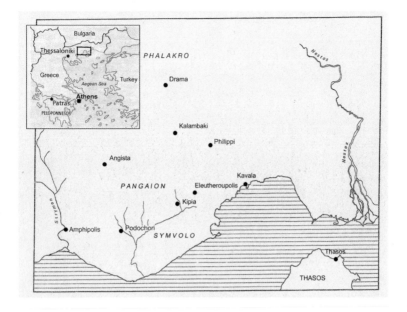

Map 1

Plan 1: *Situation before 300 CE. Width 27 meters. Length 75 meters.*

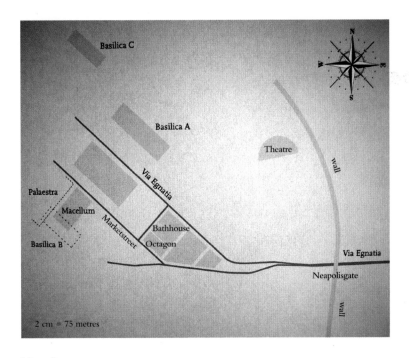

Map 2

Plan 2: *Situation circa 320 CE.* Plan 3: *Situation fifth–sixth century.*

Figure 1: *An inscription by freedmen from the first or second century.*

Figure 2: *The point where the city wall and the theatre meet.*

Figure 3: *Via Egnatia near Kavalla.*

Figure 4: *A milestone at a distance of 30 stadia from Philippi:* ΕΚ ΦΙΛΙΠΠΩΝ ΣΤΑΔΙΟΙ ΤΡΙΑΚΟΝΤΑ.

Figure 5a: *The likeness of Emperor Augustus.*

Figure 5b: *Two priests drive a plough, pulled by a cow and a bull.*

Figure 6a: *A coin from the first half of the first century with the banner of the praetorians.*

Figure 6b: *The goddess Victoria.*

Figure 7: *With this inscribed stone Philippi thanks Marcus Lollius for his activities in the town.*

Figure 8: *The Thracian king Roemetalkes II is honoured by the Roman Marcus Acculeius.*

Figure 9: *A Latin inscription in Greek letters. At the lines 2 and 3 we can decipher:* ΟΥΧΩΡΙ ΤΕΡΤΙΕ ΣΟΥΕ ΦΗΚΙΤ. *In Latin letters: uxori Tertiae suae fecit, he made [this] for his wife Tertia.*

Figure 10: *A memorial from the first century in honour of Gaius Vibius Quartus.*

Figure 12: *The priestesses of Livia Augusta, the wife of Emperor Augustus.*

Figure 11: *Tatinius Cnosus is thankful for the peace in Philippi.*

Figure 13: *An inscription made by freedmen who used to be slaves to Emperor Augustus.*

Figure 14: *An inscription by Iulius Maximus Mucianus who was allowed to wear purple on his toga.*

Figure 15: *Participants in the cult of Silvanus.*

Figure 16: *Lucius Decimius Bassus had this water well constructed in the second century.*

Figure 17: *The inscription on this sarcophagus indicates that a dinner was to be held annually in memory of the deceased.*

Figure 18: *The architrave of a monument in honour of the emperor built by Modius Laetus Rufinianus.*

Figure 19: *Identifying marks on t... steps made by construction worker...*

Figure 20: *An image of the godde... Diana in the rock.*

Figure 21: *A sanctuary in honour of Diana.*

Figure 22: *Titonius Suavis had th... stairs to the sanctuary of Isis made...*

Figure 23: *The gravestone of Symon from Smyrna.*

Figure 24: *The bottom lines of this gravestone mention a synagogue:* ΣΥ–ΝΑΓΩΓΗ.

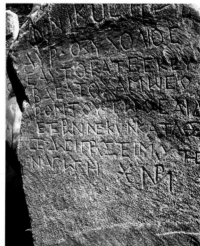

Figure 26a: *The likeness of Emperor Constans.*

Figure 26b: *The emperor standing on a galley, holding a labarum in his hand.*

Figure 25: *An inscription by order of Velleius Zosimus for men who fight wild beasts.*

Figure 27: *The subterranean tomb of Euephenes.*

Figure 28: *Bishop Porphyrius had this mosaic floor laid. The inscription starts with Porphyrius' name. Paul is mentioned at the beginning of the third line.*

Figure 29: *Detail of the floor of the Basilica of Paul.*

Figure 30: *The floor of the Octagon was laid on top of the floor of the Basilica of Paul.*

Figure 31: *The baptistery. It is clearly visible that a part of the wall was pushed back.*

Figure 32: *The water basin in the prothesis.*

Figure 33:
The gravestone of Lauricius.

Figure 34: *A cross chiselled out of the rock of the acropolis.*

Figure 35:
The gravestone of presbyter Eustathios.

Figure 36:
The gravestone of lector Aresias and his wife.

Figure 37: *A surviving wall of Basilica B.*

Figure 38: *The public latrines of the Palaestra.*

4

The second century:
a strengthening of the
Roman character of Philippi

This book has been divided into the first, second and following centuries for easy reference. However, it should be kept in mind that such a division can obscure the continuity of the facts. It is evident that the situation in the year 100 was little different from the situation one year earlier.

We have only a little information with respect to the Christian community of Philippi in the second century. An epistle by Polycarp to the Christian community of Philippi has survived, and Tertullian mentioned the church of Philippi in one of his writings at the end of the second century. We can extract more general information from inscriptions, and archaeologists have added a great deal to our knowledge over the past decades. Of course the inscriptions and the archaeological finds give information about the Christian community as well, indicating that this community had not yet stepped into the limelight. No Christians were mentioned as such in inscriptions, nor was there any construction of churches.

We will first investigate what the Epistle of Polycarp tells us about the Philippian Christian community. This epistle is much more general than Paul's. Even though Polycarp had visited Philippi and discusses some details, it does not appear that he was acquainted with many people. This is hardly surprising, because he must have spent most time in Smyrna, where he was appointed bishop. The epistle of Polycarp to the Philippians probably consists of two epistles. If this is true, these two epistles must have been merged very early on. The entire epistle as it is known today consists of 14 chapters. The thirteenth chapter is presumably a part of the older of the two epistles.

Chapter 13 makes it clear that the Philippians asked Polycarp for copies of the available epistles by Ignatius. They also requested that Polycarp forward a letter from them to the Christian congregation in Antioch. Ignatius had been the Bishop of Antioch but was arrested by the Romans. He was sentenced to death and dispatched to Rome, where he would be thrown to the beasts. His journey to Rome was via Smyrna to Troas, then to Neapolis and Philippi, and continued by the Via Egnatia. He had met Polycarp of Smyrna, and had spoken with members of the Christian community in Philippi. Apparently the Philippians had been so impressed by this meeting that they wanted to have all of Ignatius' epistles, and asked Polycarp if he possessed them. In his answer in the current chapter 13, Polycarp promised to forward their letter to Antioch and included copies of the Epistles of Ignatius which were available to him. Moreover, he asked the Philippians to pass on to him any news about Ignatius. It is evident that this Epistle of Polycarp should be dated shortly after Ignatius' departure from Philippi, but before Polycarp received the message of Ignatius' death. It is probable, then, that this epistle was written in the year 110 or shortly after.

Against this background we may assume that the Philippians collected copies of the Pauline epistles as well, as far as they could lay their hands on them. These epistles were certainly read aloud in the meetings of the Christian community. Since only a very small number of people could read and write, the community was dependent on the more literate people in order to know the contents of the epistles by Paul and Ignatius. We may imagine that the incumbents were responsible for carefully preserving this correspondence and for reading it aloud.

The second Epistle of Polycarp to the Philippians, Chapters 1–12 and 14, is usually dated in the thirties of the second century. This epistle indicates that the author knew about the sad fate of Ignatius. Chapter 9.1 speaks of 'the endurance you saw in the blessed Ignatius, Zosimus and Rufus'. This wording gives the distinct impression that the author is talking about three martyrs who had been killed for their faith.

In 11.3 and in Chapter 14 we read that Polycarp visited Philippi and that he advised the Philippians over a delicate affair. A certain Valens had been an incumbent in the Christian community of Philippi. He was a controller of finances, but he had abused his office and been guided by greed. Polycarp is very restrained in his words, but we understand from his terminology that Valens had betrayed the community's confidence. He could not keep his office any more, and the Philippians asked Polycarp for advice, as they did not know how to proceed in this matter. Polycarp appealed to the community to act very carefully and not to treat Valens as an enemy, but to move him to repent. Anyone who has been in a situation in which an official of a rather small association or community mismanaged the finances can imagine that such an incident may evoke strong responses.

This event demonstrated the problems with which a community could be confronted. It also makes it clear that the community was so small that its members could not afford to appoint a bishop of their own and had to ask the Bishop of Smyrna for help. Polycarp had visited Philippi earlier and apparently he was willing to advise and assist the community. At the same time we may conclude that the group of believers cannot have been very small. Polycarp addresses his epistle to the *church* in Philippi. This church must have been a group of believers that was identifiable as such when it decided to send a letter to the church of Antioch encouraging the believers who were deprived of their bishop. At the same time the community in Philippi was too small to appoint a delegate to Antioch. On the other hand, the request for the Epistles of Ignatius must have originated from a community that had some renown.

With the help of the numbers mentioned in chapter 2, we may assume that there would have been about 66 believers in the year 110; in the year 120, 76 people would have belonged to the Christian community. For the year 130 the estimated number of Christians in Philippi is 88 and in the year 140 the number would have increased to 101. Again, these numbers are not definitive, but they may be reconciled with the information we read in Polycarp's Epistles to the Philippians. This small community did not yet have a bishop and asked Polycarp for help. Its members wanted to send a letter to the community of Antioch, but could not dispatch this letter themselves.

Apart from the incident with Valens, there is no evidence that Polycarp had observed abuses in this community. His epistles, which were probably written about 20 years apart, paint a very positive picture of the community in Philippi. Polycarp was pleased and thankful to see the faith of the Philippians flourish and bear fruit (1.2). It may be concluded from 12.3 that the community was confronted with outside opposition. Polycarp asks the Philippians to pray for those who persecute them. This remark shows as well that this community must have been recognizable as a Christian community.

Tertullian is the other author from the second century who mentions the Christian community of Philippi. He writes at the end of the second century that the Christian communities of Philippi, Corinth, Rome and Ephesus are examples of churches where the real apostolic epistles are read and where the apostolic tradition is held in high esteem. Although such a statement does not provide much information, it makes clear that according to Tertullian the orthodox doctrine was maintained in Philippi. In all, we do not know much more about the ecclesiastical community in Philippi other than that it probably grew steadily and that Polycarp and Tertullian had no criticisms. With respect to the civil circumstances, however, we know much more.

Over the past decades archaeological research has brought to light a wealth of new information. With the help of modern methods a street plan has been determined, even for the unexcavated part of Philippi. This modern research includes, for example, the use of electrodes for measuring and mapping soil resistivity. Inscriptions from the second century give us the names of certain people and sometimes their profession as well. Huge building plans are reported for the second half of this century. None of these inscriptions makes clear that the people mentioned belonged to the church. Then again, we should not expect to find such information, as the number of Christians was very small and it was forbidden for the church to step into the limelight. If people showed themselves too obviously as Christians, they could easily get into trouble with the local administration. However, we can collect information on the basis of the published inscriptions in order to gain an insight into life in Philippi during the second century.

In the case of border disputes the administration would sometimes be asked for help. One inscription records that the border between the Philippian people and the land of an unknown person's heirs was determined anew by Emperor Hadrian. Some people are mentioned in more that one inscription. A certain Gaius Iulius Maximus Mucianus receives an honourable mention a few times. He lies buried in a sarcophagus, on which his offices have been listed. To the southeast of the forum we find another inscription with his name. It is written on a stone measuring 1.65 by 0.85 metres (Figure 14), and says among other things that he had an important administrative function in the provinces of Pontus and Bithynia, and that he was responsible for the corn supplies. The Latin phrase *latus clavus* has been used in the third and fourth lines in an inflected form. These words point to the broad purple band at the edges of his toga. Only high Roman officials were permitted to wear purple. Gaius Iulius Maximus Mucianus was allowed to do so, as he had been raised to the position of Senator by Emperor Antoninus Pius (138–161).

The name of Antoninus Pius allows us to date this inscription to the period of or shortly after his reign. However, it is often difficult to date inscriptions, because two separate systems were in use at the time. One system relates the era to the founding of the province of Macedonia in 148 BCE, but in the other system the era starts in the year 31 BCE, the year of the Battle of Actium. Sometimes it is unclear which era is used, and in some cases no year is mentioned at all. A second-century Greek epitaph, the headstone of Dionysios, the son of Dioskurides, is preserved in the museum of Serres, about 100 kilometres west of Philippi. It mentions both eras next to each other. On the basis of both eras it may be determined that this Dionysios died in the year 106 CE.

Information of a different kind is found in the lists of names of people who joined the cult of Silvanus, a Roman deity who was especially concerned with arable farming. These impressive lists, carved in stone, are readily accessible at the foot of the acropolis between the theatre and the Basilica A. Another list mentions people who contributed towards the costs of maintaining this cult of Silvanus or who donated materials for the building of a sanctuary. The inscription in Figure 15 tells us that P(ublius) Hostilius Philadelphus had this inscription made to commemorate the honour conferred upon him. The names of donors who gave presents have been listed below his name. Women were not allowed to join the cult of Silvanus. It is striking that the names mentioned here are nearly exclusively Roman. There is not a single Thracian name, and we may conclude that the cult of Silvanus was a particularly Roman affair. The rather small contributions indicate that its members were not wealthy people. Most who participated in this cult were slaves and freedmen. This might be expected, because they were the people who cultivated the land and had strong ties with agriculture. The cult involved making sacrifices to Silvanus. The Roman author Virgil tells us with regard to another city that they held a feast in honour of Silvanus every year. This may have been the case in Philippi as well. The adherents of this cult had another important purpose as well. They arranged beforehand that their burial would be well taken care of. The inscriptions mention, for example, that a certain Alfenus Aspasius, priest of Silvanus, has paid the relatively small amount of 50 *denarii* towards the costs of his burial.

The Egyptian goddess Isis was venerated among others in an inscription on a stone measuring about 1.80 by 1.10 metres. This stone may still be seen where it was found, just south of the road at the Neapolis Gate. This inscription, dating from the second or third century CE, was made by order of medical Doctor Quintus Mofius Euhemerus. It says that the doctor had an altar built at his own expense which was erected in honour of the divine house of the Emperor and was dedicated to Isis. This fascinating inscription connects the cult of the Emperor with the veneration of Isis. It also mentions that the doctor had four benches made at a place assigned by the town administration.

It is probable that Isis was venerated much earlier in Philippi. This goddess was worshipped among other things for her power to cure people. A temple in honour of Isis and other Egyptian deities had already been erected in Thessalonica in the third century BCE. It is surmised that there was once a temple in her honour in Amphipolis as well. We will see later that other inscriptions mention building activities for this goddess at the acropolis in Philippi. It is possible that the stone of Mofius Euhemerus was removed from the acropolis and used for repairs of the city wall. The Christian symbols in this stone, a dove and a cross, are of a later date.

Another inscription worth mentioning here is located at the northwest side of the forum. Two enormous blocks, each more than 2 metres wide, tell us that the water well here was constructed by order of Lucius Decimius Bassus and that it was financed from his estate (Figure 16). Lucius Decimius Bassus had been one of the *duumviri*, and he had controlled the finances of Philippi as a *quaestor*. This water well cost 30,000 *sestertii*, i.e. 7,500 *denarii*. It is difficult to estimate the value of such an amount, but the 50 *denarii* paid by Alfenus Aspasius to cover the costs of his burial shows that 7,500 *denarii* must have been a large sum of money. It is often stated that one *denarius* used to be the daily wage of a workman. If this is true, it would confirm that the construction of this well had been very expensive.

Another typically Roman office is that of *munerarius*, organizer of games. The *munerarius* arranged gladiatorial matches, or games involving wild beasts. An epitaph to a certain Publius Marius Valens informs us that he was a *munerarius* in the second half of the second century. This inscription has been lost. In Chapter 2 of this volume, I mentioned a first-century inscription in honour of Varinius Macedo, who had been a *munerarius* as well.

The tombstone of Vitalis mentions another profession. This inscription too has been lost, but fortunately the text has been preserved. Vitalis was an innkeeper for his master in the immediate vicinity of Philippi. He was a popular figure. In this inscription Vitalis asks for forgiveness if he has not given his clients the full measure. He apologizes for this, saying that this was not done in his own interest, but in his master's!

An inscription in honour of Emperor Antoninus Pius mentions several earlier emperors. They have there the predicate *divus*, divine or deified. This and other inscriptions show how emphatically emperors made their influence felt in life in the provinces. The use of the word *divus* indicates moreover that the Emperor had a place next to many other deities in the pantheon of the Roman Empire.

More people in the Philippi area had formed a sort of burial society. Some tombstones mention a specified sum of money that was provided in order to make a sacrifice on the tomb of a beloved person at the annual Rosalia celebration. This Roman festival was held when the roses were in bloom. A sarcophagus in the garden of the museum in Philippi records on one of its long sides that Zipacenthus together with others had this sarcophagus made and that Bithus and Rufus had donated money. It was their intention that a dinner be held annually at the Rosalia festival, to be paid for from the interest (Figure 17).

Naturally, such information is very fragmentary. Relatively few people had a gravestone or an inscription made, and many professions are lacking. But the inscriptions mentioned here lead us to suspect that all required amenities were available, in Philippi itself or in its immediate vicinity. Philippi had a doctor, an inn, someone who organized games, as well as several other officials who are mentioned by name. Of course it was small scale, but we do find in Philippi a reflection of national and international life.

Huge building plans were executed in the second century. The forum was completely reconstructed. Impressive buildings were erected around it. As a consequence of this and of other factors there is not much left of hellenistic Philippi. Nonetheless, due to excavations of the twentieth century, in the 1930s and 1980s, we know that there must have been a larger square. The ordinary houses around the square were pulled down to make room for the building plans of the Romans. We can draw a map of Philippi as it was constructed in the second half of the second century, showing the course of the main streets and the side streets. The housing estates were built in blocks of about 27 by 75 metres. More room was used for the construction of larger buildings.

The Via Egnatia entered the town through the Neapolis Gate, going in a westerly direction. Its trajectory may easily be seen even today. To the west of the Neapolis Gate the Via Egnatia bore off slightly the northwest, and just before this curve there was a by-road to the left. This by-road proceeded further in a westerly direction. Travelling along this street we soon see a by-road that bears off to the right, running parallel to the Via Egnatia (see Map 2, plate section). It is usually called Market Street by scholars. This name suuggests rightly that there used to be a market here. It was a food market, called a *macellum* in Latin. It was situated next to the so-called Palaestra, just south of the forum. This Palaestra was a complex where people trained for various sports, as well as performing intellectual exercises. Not much is left of the Palaestra, due to the later construction of Basilica B. The forum is located between Market Street and the Via Egnatia. People can walk here even today. Around the forum we can see the remnants of largely second-century buildings.

The enormous blocks of an architrave lie at the west side of the forum. This architrave probably belonged to a temple for the cult of the Roman Emperor. It has a clearly legible inscription, which tells us that this monument was made in honour of the imperial family and of the colony of Philippi. Gaius Modius Laetus Rufinianus was responsible for the construction of this temple. The middle of the upper line reads DIVO ANTONINO: for the divine Antoninus (Figure 18). It refers to Emperor Antoninus Pius. The second line shows the words PROVINC(IAE) MACED(ONIAE). Gaius Modius Rufinianus was *quaestor pro praetore* and *curator*. In this capacity he controlled the finances in Philippi and represented the imperial authority. This high-placed official had a temple constructed at the east side of the forum as well. It is possible that this building was intended for meetings of the administration. Big blocks of the architrave still lie on the ground. Close to the building at the east side of the forum lie stones with inscriptions that honour this official personally.

In an earlier chapter I mentioned the inscriptions for the priestesses of Livia Augusta. These first-century inscriptions have survived in spite of the second-century reconstruction of the forum. This makes it clear that the veneration of the imperial family had become very important. The buildings and these inscriptions gave the forum a clearly Roman character. Impressive fragments lie scattered all over the place. These fragments bear many inscriptions. Clearly, those people who had themselves immortalized through these precious monuments and inscriptions must have been wealthy indeed.

This century also saw the reconstruction and expansion of the theatre. The theatre had become too small as the population of Philippi increased with the Roman colonists who arrived after 42 and 31 BCE. Moreover, the Romans wanted to make the theatre fit for Roman games, which often involved wild animals. In order to protect the spectators from these animals the lower rows of seats were removed and new upper rows added. Moreover, the stage was expanded into two storeys. Several covered entrances were available for the actors and there were separate entrances for the audience in the upper rows.

The identifying marks made by construction workers on several stones are rather interesting. We can see them, for example, on the steps of the monumental staircase, north of the forum, on the northern side of the obsolete secondary road. These stairs lead to another temple. The Greek letters indicate the order of assembly of these steps (Figure 19). Standing at the bottom of these stairs and looking down we see a space consisting of two rooms on the left. Traditionally this space was believed to be the goal where Paul was imprisoned. Archaeologists have been able to determine, however, that this space was constructed by the Romans as a water reservoir. Later on the Christians converted it into a chapel. It has never been a jail.

We can find many remnants from the second century not only in the city centre, but also on the slopes of the acropolis. The most impressive are dozens of small bas-relief figurines of about 40 by 50 centimetres. These masterpieces have been hewn into the rocks. More than 90 sculptures represent Diana, goddess of the hunt (Figure 20). These 90 or so figurines represent around 50 per cent of the total number of pictures and inscriptions that have been found at the acropolis. Consequently Diana must have been incredibly important in the life of the Philippians, even though to our knowledge she was never given a temple in the town centre. Some sculptures are located very close to each other (Figure 21). These figurines are always oriented to the town, and in general are easy to reach. Even today we can find many representations of Diana here if we look for them, some of which are accompanied by an inscription as well.

One sculpture has been preserved in excellent conditions. The inscription in the stone wall next to it reads DIANE SACRUM: sanctuary of Diana. The name of the patron is mentioned beneath these words: Rutilius Maximus. Funnily enough the name of Diana has been misspelled. In this construction it should be DIANAE instead of DIANE (Figure 21). Another intriguing text is that of a priest of the Egyptian goddess Isis. It says that this priest, Lucius Titonius Suavis, had a part of the stairs to the temple constructed at his own expense. Both the inscription and some worn steps are still visible at the slope of the acropolis (Figure 22). Another inscription informs us that the same Lucius Titonius Suavis had a table and a plinth made at his own expense. In 2004 the stone with this inscription stood against the wall of the church at the cemetery of Angista, but it is certain that it originates from Philippi. Thus Isis was one of the goddesses venerated in Philippi. Other inscriptions that were found at the acropolis were dedicated to Jupiter. In the area around Philippi several inscriptions were found with his name: Iuppiter.

All this leaves us with an image of a town where many buildings were reconstructed in the second century. The Roman presence was clearly visible, especially around the forum. Large and lavish buildings show that they were wealthy and that the centre of the town was very 'Roman' in character. There was not much room left for people who wished to worship non-Roman deities. It appears that they were forced to move to the slopes of the acropolis, because the centre was monopolized by buildings used for typically Roman purposes.

The presence of Christians is not yet evident. They formed a minority group, and they must have recognized that there was no room for them in the many buildings that were constructed. They were forced to observe their celebrations quietly, without attracting attention to themselves.

This small group of Christians may have met in the houses of certain more notable persons, people with houses large enough to receive a group of Christians. Chapter 16 of Paul's Epistle to the Romans mentions the church in the house of Prisca and Aquila (Rom. 16.3-5). In Rom 16.14-15 some other people are mentioned by name as well as 'the brethren' and 'the saints', apparently other members of these groups. Such phrases point to house communities which held their celebrations in the house of a person who could accommodate them. The situation in Philippi was probably similar, and the community may have met in several smaller groups. They celebrated communion, breaking bread and serving wine. The conversations may have been related to their situation as a minority group. Theological items were certainly discussed as well at these meetings, and some kind of teaching must have taken place.

5

The third century:
largely shrouded in mist

Unfortunately we do not know of any third-century authors who wrote about the church of Philippi. We therefore need to rely upon our knowledge of the growth of Christianity in general in the Roman Empire. Inscriptions and archaeological data roughly outline life in Philippi during this century, even though there are few spectacular finds from the third century. It appears that the immense building activity of the second century culminated in a lengthy period of inactivity. Another factor was that the Roman Empire was disunited by internal dissension and anarchy in the third century, which of course must have played an important role. As a result there was much uncertainty, reducing the motivation of many people to act. By the end of the third century only Emperor Diocletian (285–305) was able to produce order out of this chaos.

As far as we know, there is no third-century archaeological find that can be related to the church of Philippi or its members. It has not yet been determined with certainty that any third-century inscription is related to a Christian. Presumably Christians had not yet made inscriptions at the time, or did not yet make it known that they were Christians. Sometimes an inscription that was made by order of a Christian has been dated in the third century, but other experts have challenged such statements and they are probably right. Only in the fourth century, when churches were built for them to meet, did Christians step into the limelight. Since then inscriptions testify that people admitted that they belonged to the Christian Church.

Earlier I outlined a sketch of a possible growth process for the church of Philippi. Of course, such a development cannot be proven, but it is plausible. If we take these numbers of growth as a guideline, the church of Philippi would have numbered about 230 members in the year 200. By the end of this century nearly 1,000 people would have belonged to the church. This is a considerable number, but clearly they were still a minority group.

It is striking that many more inscriptions from this century are in Greek compared to the two preceding centuries. Something was changing. It appears that the Romans who lived in Philippi were by then so integrated into Philippian society that they slowly but surely began to speak Greek. Nevertheless the forum was always a very Roman place. We can still see an inscription there that is dedicated to the fact that Caracalla had defeated the Germans in 213. One year later Caracalla passed through Philippi on his way to to the East. The memorial was probably erected in honour of Caracalla's visit to Philippi. An inscription on a very simple tombstone, dated in the same century, consists of just two words: Simon Smyrnaios. This stone stands in the garden of the museum (Figure 23). It is not very informative, but it confirms that there were contacts between Philippi and Asia Minor, and more specifically between Philippi and Smyrna. Lydia, mentioned in Acts 16, originally came from Asia Minor, and in the second century the Christians in Philippi had had contacts with Polycarp, Bishop of Smyrna, who had helped them solve some problems.

Perhaps an inscription that mentions a synagogue must be dated during the third century as well. This inscription was found at the western cemetery. It says that Flavius Nikostratos Aurelius Oxycholios built this tomb and that everybody who buries another person in this tomb must pay a fine to the synagogue (Figure 24). The significance of this inscription is that it demonstrates the presence of Jews in Philippi. This is the first time after the remark in Acts 16.13 that such a statement is made. The mention of a synagogue demonstrates that the number of Jews must have been larger than in the time when the Book of Acts was written. The fine that had to be paid would benefit the synagogue. In other inscriptions it is decreed that another sum of money was to be paid to the person who had seen the offence and had brought the charge.

An altar that was constructed by order of Valeria Mantana is interesting as well. We read at this altar that she had it built for her husband Aurelius Zipyron Dizas and herself. Her husband's names betray his Thracian origin. The continuation of this inscription also shows that there were ties between them and Thracia: Valeria Mantana had paid a certain amount of money to the funerary association of the Thracian deity Suregethes. A sacrifice was to be made each year and its costs were to be paid from the interest. If the association did not meet its obligations it had to pay a fine – twice the amount – to the rival association of the Thracian Horseman!

A splendid stone 0.44 metres wide and more than twice as high forms a part of the entrance to the theatre. Two inscriptions and pictures were chiselled into this stone by order of Marcus Velleius Zosimus. They inform us that he had the pictures and the inscriptions made for the association of men who fought wild beasts. Such combats were favourite public games for the Romans. One inscription is accompanied by a picture of Nike, as always portrayed with broad wings (Figure 25). Mars, the Roman god of war, is pictured next to the other inscription.

We see, then, that in the third century Philippi still clearly had the marks of the groups of colonists who had settled there in the first century BCE, but the Greek language was used more frequently than before. The integration of the Romans into Philippian society started to become visible. Typically Roman events such as combats with wild beasts were still popular with many people, but the language of the Romans faded out in this part of Greece.

In religious matters we still see much variation, even though there is no evidence of Christianity in any inscription that can be dated to the third century with certainty. But things were about to change.

6

The fourth century: plenty of room for Christians

We know much more about the fourth century and the two following centuries with respect to the church than we know about the second and the third centuries. The fourth century saw many events in the Roman Empire that are of major importance for church history.

First, the role of the future Emperor Constantine the Great should be mentioned here. Before he became Emperor he had to fight many enemies. According to Christian tradition Constantine had a vision the night before a very important battle in 313. In this vision he saw the Christogram, i.e. the first two Greek letters of the name of Christ. Next to it was a text that could be translated as follows: 'In this sign you will be the victor.' Constantine defeated his enemies and after he had conferred with Licinius, with whom he shared authority at the time, he officially commanded full tolerance of Christianity and gave it the same rights as other religions. Constantine's decision did not mean that he had become a Christian overnight. The triumphal arch erected for him near the Colosseum in Rome is still there, and here we read that he had gained victory *instinctu divinitatis, mentis magnitudine*: by divine inspiration and by his own great spirit. Although these words do not really witness a conversion to Christianity, nevertheless more room was now given to Christians.

Constantine's decision had huge consequences. Until then the Christians, who constituted about 10 per cent (i.e. about 6 million people) of the population of the Roman Empire had not been allowed to build a sanctuary or even a place to meet. Nor had they been allowed to step into the limelight. It is true that there had been no wide-scale or protracted persecutions, but the situation whereby Christians were just tolerated was far from comfortable.

It is clear that the influence of Christians increased rapidly following Constantine's decision. Conversely it is also clear that the government began to exert influence on the church from this time onwards. Interfering more and more in matters of the church, Constantine himself convened the so-called first ecumenical council in Nicea, present-day Iznik in the west of Turkey, in 325. A short while later he made Byzantium the capital of his empire. He called this city Constantinople, city of Constantine, after himself. It is sometimes suggested that the current name Istanbul is a corruption of Constantinople, but other derivations of this name are possible as well. The inauguration of Constantinople was magnificently celebrated in the year 330.

Moving the capital to the east was a far-reaching decision. Of course this was very harmful for Rome, which had been the capital of the Roman Empire up until then. However, the seat of the most influential bishop at that time did remain in Rome.

The Emperor himself brought Christianity more and more into the limelight. Very soon the Christogram, the so-called labarum, appeared on many coins. In Figures 26a and 26b we see the portrait of Emperor Constans, the son of Constantine the Great. On the reverse the emperor is pictured standing on a galley, holding a labarum in his hand. Developments gained momentum. In the middle of the fourth century the number of Christians had grown to 50 per cent of the population of the Empire. Consequently they could assume power. There were efforts by Julian, called the Apostate, to reinstate the non-Christian religions during his short government, but he failed in this endeavour. Emperor Theodosius called a definitive halt to all uncertainty in 380 by declaring that Christianity would be the state religion from that time on, effectively taking away the rights of all non-Christian religions. He put an end to the constrained freedom of religion in former decades, obliging every citizen of the Roman Empire to join

Christianity. This must have led to great uncertainty for those with different views. A well-known teacher like Libanius in Antioch was not embarrassed, apparently. However, when it became forbidden in 391 to visit temples and make sacrifices, spontaneous riots broke out and heathen temples were destroyed. Archaeological research has showed that the sanctuary of the Thracian Horseman in Kipia in the Philippian territory, for example, was devastated during that period.

What was happening in Philippi at this time? There are no accounts of Christians spontaneously celebrating when the decision by Constantine was made known, but we can well imagine that they were very happy with this development. Shortly after the decision to allow Christianity had been made, the Christians in Philippi started to build their first church, slightly to the east of the forum. A wide street with columns runs from the Via Egnatia, just below the obsolete secondary road. After about 70 metres on the left, we see the remnants of the churches which succeeded each other. We will deal with these churches at some greater length below.

In Chapter 1 of this volume, I mentioned that next to other deities a certain Euephenes was venerated in Philippi. Euephenes was a priest of the Kabeiroi. In a sketch I indicate the place where the heroon, the memorial shrine of Euephenes, was situated (see Plan 1). We can still walk in the columned street from the Via Egnatia to the Roman bath house, which is on the left. The room after that, thus just south of the bath house, was a storage room, and after that we see the remnants of the sanctuary. The subterranean burial chamber is still there (Figure 27), but cannot be visited any more after an accident occurred some years ago. The burial chamber is dated to the second century BCE. There was a small shrine above the burial chamber. A kind of courtyard surrounding it belonged to the territory of the sanctuary. The Christians built a so-called basilica in the southern part of this courtyard, probably in the 320s. This basilica was about 25 metres long and nearly 10 metres wide on the inside (see Plan 2). At the east side of the nave of this church we can see a copy of an inscription that gives us the name of this church, informing us that Bishop Porphyrius had the mosaic floor laid in this 'Basilica of Paul' (Figure 28). The original inscription may be seen in the museum. Porphyrius signed the attendance lists at the synod of Sardica, present-day Sofia, in

342/343 in his function as Bishop of Philippi. Archaeologists have determined that the mosaic floor was put in some time after the church was built, so the construction of the church may be dated one or two decades earlier.

The word *basilica* originally described a simple rectangular building used for public meetings. One of the short sides usually contained an apse. A judge or other high official could be in session there. It is remarkable that the courtyard of the heroon was used for the construction of this basilica. This event allows us to state that the Christians were free to act then and the believers apparently did not object to the fact that their first church would be built on the holy ground around the sanctuary of Euephenes. The northern wall of the basilica was the southern wall of the heroon. There was a door that allowed access from the heroon to the church and vice versa. A large part of the beautiful original mosaic floor (Figure 29) has been exposed. Besides the inscription mentioned above it has a Greek inscription that is oriented to be legible for people entering the church from the heroon. It reads 'Lord, help your servant Priscus and all his family'. Are we supposed to conclude, then, that some people joined both the Christian meetings in the basilica and the cult at the heroon? It looks like it, and we will see that the later history of this church shows that both sanctuaries were closely connected in later times as well.

The Basilica of Paul burned down at the end of the fourth century, but the Christians started building a new church shortly afterwards. Some scholars believe that this new church was already built in the fourth century, but others stated that its construction was started at the beginning of the fifth century. This new church was built as an Octagon (see Plan 3). The site southwest of the Basilica of Paul was prepared for building as well and the Octagon was built in the centre of the available room, leaving room to walk around it on all sides. The new floor of the Octagon lay at a higher level than the old mosaic floor of Paul's Basilica (Figure 30). We can see enough of both floors to picture what they originally looked like. Additional rooms were constructed, but care was taken to leave the shrine of Euephenes intact. We can still see remnants of the walls which separated the rooms. Plan 3 clearly shows that the rooms with the numbers I–VIII were constructed around the sanctuary. In addition, the storage room of the bath house was sacrificed for these additional rooms. The wall on the north side is still the ancient wall that separated the storage room from the bath house, but the wall on the north side of room V, where people were baptised, was partly pulled down. A new wall was erected slightly further to the north, in order to create a square room. In the middle of this room a square baptistery was built in the shape of a cross. Today visitors can observe the new wall to the north of room V, and they can see this baptistery very clearly. Figure 31 shows the cross-shaped baptistery and the new wall, looking to the northeast.

What would have been the function of the older Hellenistic sanctuary during these years? Room VII has been identified as a 'diaconicon', or sacristy. This room held a large stone water reservoir, which is still there. Notches in the wall and surviving parts of earthenware water pipes show that a water pipe ran from the bath house into the reservoir. Another pipe led some of the water to a lower round basin in the prothesis, the room for the offerings (room VIII; see Figure 32). A hole in the bottom of the big stone reservoir served to drain the excess water. From this hole a pipe led to a large drain. There were many coins found in these rooms. They were probably donated by people who entered the prothesis with their offerings and left with a little holy water from the basin, probably in a flask. This water had passed through the stone reservoir in the diaconicon and was stored in the round basin, which had given it surplus value. Many such flasks have been found at the tombs of martyrs in Egypt, in present-day Jordan and elsewhere. A similar ritual with holy water appears to be the most evident explanation for the archaeological finds here, even if such flasks have not been found in Philippi until now.

The question remains as to the process that made the water holy. In Abu Mina in Egypt, in Seleucia in present-day Turkey and, for example, in Thessalonica, Christians held rituals during which water or oil became holy through the presence of a martyr's body or other relics. People were convinced that such liquids possessed healing properties. Is it possible that Paul, after whom the first church was called, had been given the role of Euephenes and that he was venerated? Some scholars even assume that the church of Philippi possessed some relics of Paul, but we do not have any evidence for this claim. It seems certain to me that some sort of ritual with holy water must have taken place around the tomb and that this was the reason why the ancient burial chamber was left intact.

The cult of Euephenes has probably been adopted by the Christians with some adaptations. The holy ground around the burial chamber of Euephenes was where the church was built and where the Christians met for their celebrations. The building was partly maintained and the rituals were continued in an adapted form by the Christians. Of course, the name of Euephenes was no longer mentioned, but it is very probable that Paul's name was connected with this cult. After all, the first church was called Paul's Basilica, and according to Acts 16 Paul had baptised the first converts of Europe in Philippi. They must have felt a strong bond with him.

Another church was built during this century, the so-called *Basilica extra muros*, the Basilica outside the walls. As its name tells us, this basilica is not located in the centre of ancient Philippi but outside it, to the east of the Neapolis Gate in the centre of the present-day village of Krenides. There is a fence around it, but it may be seen from the footpath. The church has not been completely excavated, because this would require the streets to be broken up and inhabited houses to be pulled down. But coins and inscriptions found here make it clear that this church, a cemetery basilica, was constructed in the first half of the fourth century. Many tombs have been found here, from earlier centuries as well. But from the fourth century onward Christians systematically buried their dead here, and this church was constructed for their burial rituals.

From this time onward the surviving inscriptions show the presence of Christians in Philippi. It is striking that the number of Latin inscriptions dwindled. Greek was used more and more and the Roman character of Philippi faded into the background. I know of only two Latin inscriptions from Christians. One of them says, *Hic in pac(e requiescit) in nomine Ch(risti) Lauricius (servus Dei) qui vixit an(nos XXII)*: 'here rests in peace in the name of Christ, Lauricius, servant of God, who has lived 22 years'. I have completed the words that were abbreviated or that are no longer there. This stone was found at the Basilica extra muros. It may now be admired in the garden of the museum (Figure 33).

During this time inscriptions were made that include the name Kyriakos. This name points to the word Kyrios, Lord, the title that was given to Christ. One inscription from the fourth century informs us that a teacher with the name Kyriakos had this tomb made for himself, for his wife Aurelia Marcellina and for his children. Kyriakos and his family were buried in a cemetery east of Philippi. Other inscriptions sometimes mention not only the name of the deceased but also his or her office in the church. One inscription mentions a presbyter, an elder, Aurelius Capiton, who belonged to the 'catholic church'. He had this gravestone with its inscription made for his parents, his wife and his son. Another gravestone has been found at the grave of the presbyters Faustinus and Donatus, 'presbyters in the catholic, apostolical, holy church of the Philippians'. Another presbyter, a doctor, was named after Paul. Another find is a grave that belonged to Deaconess Posidonia and Canon Pancharia. It cannot be determined with certainty if this last inscription originates from the fourth or the fifth century. All these inscriptions show that the number of offices saw a sharp increase during these centuries.

It may have been felt in those days that tensions arose in the church between different groups. An inscription has been found in a burial chamber, and it says: 'Lord have mercy on us and raise us up who passed away in the true, orthodox faith.' These last words probably indicate that there were dissidents as well in Philippi. Some scholars argue on the basis of such an inscription that the presence of Arianists in Philippi can be stated. That is not at all certain, but the words 'the true faith' indicate that people in Philippi knew of controversies that had attracted attention in the fourth-century church. Bishop Porphyrios must certainly have discussed this in his church. It is likely that not everyone in Philippi was equally interested in theological subtleties, but Porphyrios' presence at the synod of Sardica means that he was involved, and we know that he took the 'orthodox' position there.

At the Council of Nicea in 325 it had been decided that Christ was *homo-ousios* with the Father, meaning of the same substance as the Father. This decision clashed with the opinion of the Arianists, who denied that Christ was God. According to them, only the Father was God. They considered Christ to be the highest creature. Arius was exiled at the Council of Nicea, but this did not mean that his points of view were no longer held. The decision of Nicea was adopted quite generally in the west of Europe, but in the east people were reluctant to be told what to believe by the Bishop of Rome and the Emperor. There too the so-called orthodox point of view was often rejected.

The same problems were discussed at the synod of Sardica. Things went smoothly for the bishops in attendance, because the Arianists withdrew from the synod and the orthodox point of view could easily be confirmed. Porphyrius, Bishop of Philippi, signed the attendance lists and he agreed with the orthodox point of view. Perhaps we can deduce from this that the church of Philippi joined the majority point of view in this respect. If so, the reference to the 'orthodox belief' on the gravestone would indicate which opinion was adopted by the people mentioned on it.

A very different inscription has been found between the forum and Basilica B. This was the area where the shops were located. One of the shopkeepers, a butcher, had scratched a segmented circle in the stone in front of his shop. In this circle and the segments he wrote his name and his profession: butcher John. The letters are barely legible, but the circle is still clearly visible. This circle acted as a board for a game played with pieces or discs in two colours. The name John indicates that this butcher was a Christian, and this is confirmed by two crosses inside the circle. We can find similar circles there, but they are smaller and they do not have inscriptions.

Thus we gain a picture of a tempestuous development that took place in the fourth century. At first, the Christians were allowed to openly admit to their belief and to observe their celebrations. Later on Christianity even became the only religion that was permitted. We saw that enormous building activities were undertaken in Philippi and elsewhere in the Roman Empire. Many churches were built throughout the Empire. From that time onward Christians were allowed to occupy high offices. In the second half of the fourth century the Christians even gained control of the government of the entire empire.

7

The fifth century:
the church is obviously
present in Philippi

The introduction of Christianity as a state religion in 380 had effects in the following centuries as well. Every person was now supposed to be a Christian. The government contributed generously towards the costs of the construction of many churches in the Roman Empire. We will see that still more churches would be built in Philippi and that Christianity had a prominent place in other ways as well. Even today we can still see a cross on the slope of the acropolis. It has been chiselled out of the rock, slightly to the east of the museum at the border of the zigzagging path to the top. First we see some second-century pictures of Diana/Artemis, and then we pass the cross, right at the end of that part of the twisting path, and before the scant remnants of the temple of the Egyptian goddess Isis. This cross measures 56 by 43 centimetres (Figure 34). It is as if the cross may have served to neutralize the images of the non-Christian gods and may in some way have christianized the entire slope of the acropolis.

In the second half of this century it became increasingly clear that Philippi was threatened from the north and that there were not enough Roman soldiers available any more to avert this threat. In 473 Philippi was besieged by the Goths. Although this siege ended in failure, it was a forerunner of the raids from the north. Such raids would occur again and again. In spite of these dangers Philippi was nonetheless still a lively provincial town at this time.

The so-called Basilica A was probably built by the end of this century. We know only the name of Paul's Basilica. Therefore the archaeologists called the other churches that were excavated Basilica A, Basilica B and Basilica C. These churches received their names in the order of their excavation, which does not reflect the order of their construction date! This was common practice. In Amphipolis, for example, we also find churches that are named Basilica A, Basilica B and so on. Archaeologists have found another church in Philippi, in the west of the walled town. This church, which has been called Basilica D for the time being, has not been excavated yet.

Basilica A is situated north of the Via Egnatia, just above the secondary road that runs straight across ancient Philippi. This is a very large basilica. Measuring 55 by 27 metres, including the narthex, this church was wider than the length of Paul's Basilica! Assuming that a space of 1 square metre was required per person, over 1,000 people could attend divine service here. Moreover, this church had a gallery as well. Rows of columns divided the church into three parts. The plan of the ground floor is easily recognized. Accordingly the apse can clearly be seen. A big stone slab in the nave marks the place where the pulpit once stood. Beautifully chiselled stones stood upright between the columns. Some remnants of these stones may now be seen in the museum.

We know the names of two bishops of Philippi from this century: Flavianus and Sozon. We have some knowledge of their opinions owing to their presence at ecclesiastical meetings. We may assume that the majority of the community that was led by them held the same views. Flavianus was bishop at the beginning of the fifth century. Popes Innocentius I (401–417) and Coelestinus (422–432) wrote several letters regarding theological problems to ecclesiastical officials during these years. It is striking that Flavianus was one of the addressees. Although he was bishop in a small town, he must nevertheless have been held in high esteem. In 431 he attended the Council of Ephesus, which was convened by Emperor Theodosius II. The fact that Flavianus replaced Bishop Rufus of Thessalonica here also indicates that Flavianus enjoyed a certain status, because up until then the Bishop of Philippi had never been asked to fill in for the Bishop of Thessalonica if the latter could not attend a meeting. Flavianus spoke more than once at the Council of Ephesus. He had strong points of view and he could express them very well. The most important item on the agenda at this council was the question whether Mary should be called 'Mother of God'. At earlier councils it had been emphasized time and again that Jesus was also God. The ultimate consequence of this statement was bound to be that Mary was the Mother of God. But this conclusion was unacceptable for Nestorius, patriarch of Constantinople. Nestorius argued that the two natures of Jesus, namely his divine nature and his human nature, were so separate that some elements of Jesus' life belonged to the human being Jesus, while other aspects related to the fact that he was God as well. Pope Coelestinus had written to Flavianus that Nestorius's viewpoint should be condemned, Flavianus agreed. Eventually the council decided in accordance with the Pope's statements: Jesus was both God and a human being, and it was impossible to separate the two; consequently Mary was rightly called Mother of God. Nestorius was condemned.

In the middle of the fifth century a certain Sozon was Bishop of Philippi. We do not know any more about this Sozon than what is laid down in the reports of the Synod of Ephesus (449) and the Council of Chalcedon (451). The Octagon may have been expanded during his administration, but this is not certain. The viewpoint of a certain Eutyches, who was held in high regard in Alexandria, was discussed at the Synod of Ephesus. Eutyches had been present at the Council of Ephesus in 431 and had condemned Nestorius' viewpoint. Later on he placed so much emphasis on the fact that Jesus was also God that according to some the human nature of Jesus was no longer validated. Apparently Eutyches taught that Jesus had not really been a human being.

Besides this theological debate there was also a struggle for power between the schools of Alexandria and Constantinople. At the Synod of Ephesus Alexandria managed to force a vote by enlisting the help of armed groups of monks. This vote worked out in favour of Eutyches and caused Pope Leo the Great to dub this synod a 'Robber Synod'. Amid this tumultuous situation Bishop Sozon of Philippi declared Eutyches' viewpoint in agreement with the doctrine of the church. Only two years later another council was held, this time in Chalcedon, a stone's throw from Constantinople. The Council of Chalcedon was convened by Marcianus, who had succeeded Emperor Theodosius II. The influence of Marcianus and his wife Pulcheria was great. The imperial couple wanted to have Eutyches' viewpoints condemned, also at the Pope's request. And so, only two years after the Church Fathers had agreed with the statements of Eutyches – albeit under duress – they condemned his viewpoint. Bishop Sozon of Philippi attended both meetings. It seems very likely that in 449 he approved the viewpoint of Eutyches in spite of himself. As far as we know the bishops of Philippi always took the orthodox position, as did most bishops in that part of the Roman Empire. It is most probable that Sozon always defended the 'official' orthodox viewpoints in his community in Philippi as well.

According to one tradition Sozon is the founder of the monastery of Kosfinitsa, which is situated high up in the Pangaion mountains. Other traditions however date this monastery to a later period. The isolated monastery may be reached via a road that is difficult to negotiate by car. A visit is certainly worth the effort.

Inscriptions that may be dated to this century mention several individuals who had been assigned tasks in the church. We read, for example, that a tomb belonged to a certain Paul, who was the head (literally: the first) of the presbyters in the 'holy church of God of the Philippians'. This stone was found at the Basilica extra muros, the cemetery basilica in the centre of present-day Krenides. Unfortunately it had fallen to pieces, but the stone has been restored and may be viewed at the Philippi museum. The tombstone of the presbyter Eustathios is still lying on the floor of the Basilica extra Muros (Figure 35). The Greek word for tomb has been abbreviated and the name Eustathios is represented by a monogram consisting of the first four letters of Eustathios' name. Another tombstone that was found here mentions a certain Andreas, *tribunus notariorum*. He died when only 18 years old. The title *tribunus notariorum* indicates a high office at court. We may think of a position of confidence, such as offices of diplomats, legal experts and so on. Andreas probably came from a distinguished family and was given this title in advance, as it is very unlikely that he filled this position aged 18. The deaconess Agathe and the linen weaver John were buried at the Basilica extra muros as well. It was John's task to administer the church finances. As a linen weaver he may have made the vestments for the bishops of Philippi.

Another profession mentioned in the inscriptions is that of architect. The architect Alexander lies buried in a tomb in which his wife and his mother are also buried. It is very probable that Alexander assisted in the repair and the extensions of the churches. Another stone mentions a woman called Theodora. She was married to a *centurion*, a leader of 100 soldiers. He was called Agrykios. Her tombstone lies in the atrium of Basilica B. In the narthex of this church lies the tombstone of the 'very pious lector Aresias and his wife' (Figure 36). This stone measures 93 by 67 centimetres. Aresias was responsible for the lectures in church. The name of his wife is not mentioned. In the west cemetery a stone was found with the name of a certain Andreas, 'the very humble lector.' This stone is now lost.

To the north of Philippi, in a village that belongs to its territory, winepresses and wine vessels have been found. The name Andreas may be read beside a christogram on the potsherd of a wine vessel. We can only wonder whether Andreas owned a winepress or just stored his wine there. Perhaps he supplied the wine for the dinners that the Christians celebrated together. In any case this potsherd indicates that the Christians participated in public life in all respects. Since Christianity had become a state religion in 380 all sorts of profane matters were labelled with Christian symbols. Such an inscription shows that the Christians made themselves known as Christians, for example, by using such a christogram.

A text of an entirely different nature is the so-called exchange of letters between Abgar and Jesus, but it is as fascinating as some inscriptions mentioned above. This lengthy text was found at the Neapolis Gate at the beginning of the twentieth century. Its carrier was lost, but fortunately the text has been preserved. The first part of this pseudepigraphic correspondence purports to be a letter from Abgar, king of the realm of Osroene, to Jesus. Abgar lived in Edessa, the capital of his realm. A leper, he asks Jesus to cure him. The second part is Jesus' answer. He says that he will not come, but will send someone in his place. The last sentences of this epistle promise peace, saying that the city will not fall into enemy hands. These last words have made towns such as Ephesus, Philippi and others consider this text as a protection against harm. The text may be read at the Neapolis Gate in Philippi. Another, similar inscription has been found at the Neapolis Gate. Two surviving fragments are kept in the museum. In this inscription Jesus Christ, 'born of the virgin Mary and crucified on our behalf', is asked to help the town and to protect those living there.

We see, then, that people from all strata of society are mentioned in these inscriptions which must most probably be dated to the fifth century. It is not surprising that many people mentioned that they belonged to the church. Christianity had become a state religion and there was no need for anyone to be afraid to make it known that they were Christians. In contrast, it was the non-Christian religions that were forbidden. The bishops of Philippi attended several synods and councils, and they always represented the 'orthodox' viewpoints. The only exception was Bishop Sozon's vote at the so-called Robber Synod, but this vote was made under duress. To our knowledge only one church was constructed during this century: the Basilica A, but the number of churches would soon increase. The raid of the Goths from the north shows that the Romans were no longer in a position to protect their citizens living in border regions from raids and looting by other peoples.

8

The sixth century:
the Christian character of
Philippi is reinforced

Compared with other centuries, we have a wealth of information with respect to the sixth century. Around the year 530 Bishop Demetrios was head of the church of Philippi. Demetrios is well known because of the orders he had to carry out for Emperor Justinian elsewhere, but he was very active in Philippi as well. A great deal was happening with respect to the construction or extension of churches, and archaeologists have been able to reconstruct several building activities. The threat from the north increased during this century. In particular, raids from Slav peoples now frightened the inhabitants of cities such as Thessalonica and Philippi. But the Philippians were not yet prepared to leave the area.

As was mentioned in the previous chapter, the huge church that is called Basilica A was built shortly before the year 500. Soon after another church was erected, at a distance of about 100 metres from Basilica A. This new church was excavated after Basilica B and is therefore called Basilica C. Excavation activities have not yet been completed, and for this reason the church has been fenced off, but we can walk along it and get a good impression. The plan of this church can be easily made out. A beautiful floor with small marble inlays can be seen in a room on the north side. The stone foundation for the pulpit still lies in the centre of the nave. At the northwest edge part of the stairs can be seen. The stairs led to the gallery. The precise length of this church cannot be known, because the western part of the church lies underneath the museum, but it is certain that this church is much smaller than Basilica A.

Basilica C was presumably expanded in the 530s. More annexes were built and a second pulpit was added. This second pulpit was only accessible from the apse, and so apparently was intended only for the incumbents. This is all the more striking because at the same time a second pulpit was added to the Octagon as well, during a radical restoration. It is possible that the bishop in charge intended to honour the eastern tradition by adding pulpits in this manner. In Palestine, Syria and elsewhere, the pulpit was usually located close to the altar, whereas in the West the pulpit was often the centre of the church. The restorations of these churches are dated to the initial period of Emperor Justinian (527–565), i.e. the time that Demetrios was bishop in Philippi. This dating has been done on the basis of coins that have been found there. It has recently been argued that in two churches in Thessalonica there were also two pulpits in use at the beginning of the seventh century, and perhaps earlier.

A little later another church was built, this one to the south of the forum. Archaeologists have called this enormous church Basilica B. Clearly, the influence of Christianity continued to increase. The construction of this new church even required the demolition of part of the Palaestra. Times had changed, and there was no longer any need for an institute for martial arts. Basilica B was 56 metres long, including the narthex, and 28 metres wide. The impressive remnants of the large pillars may be seen from far away (Figure 37). In contrast with the older basilicas, this basilica's nave was square, with a round dome above it. This new building type for churches was in fashion in the 530s, and was applied in Constantinople by architects, but it caused many problems. The Church of Sergius and Bacchus, also known as the Small Hagia Sophia, is still standing, but this is due to the fact that its dome rests upon an octagon. The dome of the Hagia Sophia in Constantinople rested upon a square, and it collapsed within 30 years of its construction. It had to be restored and supported time and again. The dome of the adjacent Hagia Irene was constructed during the same period. It too collapsed and had to be rebuilt. Things were even worse for Basilica B in Philippi. The dome collapsed during its construction, and the basilica was never completed. Nevertheless, its remains are very impressive. The capitals on the columns are magnificent, and remind us of the capitals in Constantinople's Hagia Sophia. It is assumed that the master builders in Philippi are pupils or co-workers of the two master builders of the Hagia Sophia, namely Anthemius of Tralles and Isidorus of Miletus. Although this cannot be proved, the similarities are striking. The construction of Basilica B is dated to the middle of the sixth century, only 15 years after the consecration of the Hagia Sophia in Constantinople.

As yet nothing can be said about the so-called Basilica D, simply because this church has not yet been excavated. All we know is where it is located (i.e. to the west of the forum), but at present even its date cannot be given.

It is certain, then, that three churches were built in Philippi within 50 years, in the chronological order of Basilica A, Basilica C and Basilica B. Moreover, there already was a church, that which is usually called the Octagon. This number of churches is in no way proportional to the number of worshippers, but in itself this is not a unique phenomenon. Five churches have been excavated in Amphipolis, about 60 kilometres west of Philippi, and these churches were even closer together. As was the case in Philippi, these churches were constructed within a short period of time.

The construction of churches in Philippi, Amphipolis and elsewhere was partly due to the intentions of wealthy members of the church. They probably thought it an honour to have a church built, just as in preceding centuries rich Romans had temples built for their gods and their Emperor, or even had monuments built for themselves. Moreover, it also happened that wealthy people had a church constructed in order to thank God. It is said, for example, that the Hagios Demetrios church in Thessalonica was erected by order of a certain Leontios in gratitude for being cured. Another major financial contributor to the construction of churches was the government. In this manner many churches could be built.

The function of the Octagon was not just to be a meeting place for the congregation. In this respect it differed from the other churches. Obviously church members met in the Octagon as well, but they came to the Octagon especially to offer donations and to share in the blessings of the 'holy water', which was supposed to contain special powers due to the assumed vicinity of the body or of relics of a deceased martyr. Be this as it may, it is striking that so many churches were built in Philippi and elsewhere in such a short time.

I have already mentioned the name of Bishop Demetrios. This bishop was very active on many levels, so much so that one might ask how much time he had left to spend on the church of Philippi. It was probably in 531 that he was involved in the preparation of ecclesiastical meetings. Together with Bishop Hypatius of Ephesus he worked on the preparation of an assembly in Constantinople. This assembly was an opportunity for orthodox bishops and monophysites to consult under the watchful eye of a high official of the Emperor. Emperor Justinian strove to bring the dissent in the church to an end in order to strengthen the unity in his empire, but he was unsuccessful. The monophysites, who argued that Christ had a single nature, opposed the pronouncements of the Council of Chalcedon in 451, which had decreed that Jesus was both God and a human being, and that these natures could not be changed, divided or separated. The problem was that these statements led to new debates time and again. Justinian tried to find the golden mean that would be acceptable to both the monophysites and the adherents of Chalcedon's decrees. In 533 Demetrios and Hypatius were sent to Rome by the Emperor. Their task was to convince Pope John II to support Justinian in his attempts to restore unity in the church. Pope John II agreed with Justinian's mediation, but these efforts failed as well. The monophysites were unrelenting.

Demetrios and Hypatius had a political mission as well. The Goths had assumed power in Rome, and Justinian was trying to regain power for the Roman Empire in the city. Demetrios and Hypatius were ordered to enter into secret negotiations with Theodahad, who intended to depose the Gothic queen Amalasuntha. But Justinian's efforts did not lead to lasting success.

Apart from all these activities Bishop Demetrios managed to work in Philippi as well. His influence may still be seen. The renovation of Basilica C and the construction of a second pulpit there, as well as a radical renovation of the Octagon and the construction of its second pulpit can all be dated to the time of Demetrios. Some scholars argue that the construction of Basilica B started in his time too, but this seems much less probable. In any case, it is clear that Demetrios left his mark on ecclesiastical life in Philippi. He had good contacts at the court of Justinian, which is possibly the reason why he had access to money to embellish the churches in Philippi. His familiarity with Constantinople and the construction of churches there may have led to the many similarities with the construction and furnishing of the churches in Philippi. Bishop Demetrios was obviously a driving force. He was active on several levels and he was of major importance to the churches in Philippi.

Several Greek inscriptions dating from this century mention officials. One inscription on a tomb informs us that the presbyter Peter is buried there, adding that anybody who places another body in this tomb will have to give an account to God, here in this place and on Judgment Day. Virtually the same formulation may be read on the tomb of presbyter Stephanos. These tombs and more have been found at a cemetery in the village of Kipia at the foot of the Pangaion mountains, to the west of the lively town of Eleutheroupolis. This area once belonged to the territory of Philippi as well. A tombstone of a certain Cyprianos has been found in another village. He was buried there with his wife, who was probably called Mary. The inscription on the stone states that 'Our Lord Jesus Christ rules as a King'.

In conclusion, we can state that many buildings were constructed in the sixth century for the benefit of the Christian community. The number of churches was rather disproportional for such a small community. Moreover, these churches were very close together. A large amount of money was spent on the embellishment of these churches. Bishop Demetrios left his mark on the construction of churches, and on their layout and design. Christianity was emphatically present everywhere. But from a political viewpoint the situation became increasingly threatening. The number of raids from the north increased and there was no longer sufficient protection against the intruders.

9

Philippi:
the final chapter

In the seventh century and later life became increasingly difficult in and around Philippi. The hostilities from the north and several earthquakes caused more and more people to move away from Philippi. A series of earthquakes occurring between the years 615 and 620 in the area between the island of Thasos, Thessalonica and Skopje in the present-day Republic of Macedonia caused huge devastation. It is also documented that during that period the population of Thasos left the town and settled elsewhere. The earthquakes damaged many buildings in Philippi, and they were a recurring nightmare. The inhabitants of Philippi were ready to leave. However, these events did not happen overnight, and it would take a few centuries before the town was completely deserted.

Even today the ruins still show that a small church was built inside the huge space of Basilica B. Its apse can easily be recognized due east of the surviving wall of Basilica B. The small church may be dated to the ninth or tenth century. It shows that the Christians could no longer afford the erection of large, new churches. Moreover, this small church offered enough space for the dwindling numbers of worshippers. Recurring raids from the north were frightening experiences. In the tenth century there was a temporary and short revival of the Roman Empire, but it was of little consequence to Philippi. The dangers posed by the Slav people and by other nearby peoples were persistent. For these various reasons people left Philippi in the hope of building a better life elsewhere. The ruins were left behind, bearing witness to the captivating history of a town and its church community.

10

A walk through Philippi

Some places in Philippi have been mentioned repeatedly in this chronological discussion of the most important events in the church history of Philippi. A different approach is also possible, with the geography of the town as a starting point. In this chapter I will discuss the monuments in the area in geographical order. To find out more information about a particular monument I suggest you leaf back to the discussion of the century in which it was constructed.

I will start with the village of Krenides. The remnants of the Basilica extra muros are located in the centre of the village, in a public garden. This church, which was built in the fourth century CE, was intended for meetings with regard to burials. Walking east across the shopping street next to the public garden, leaving the town and continuing for about 2 kilometres, you will come upon the large first-century stone bearing the name of Gaius Vibius Quartus. This road is where the ancient Via Egnatia used to be. The memorial was erected here to be seen by everyone who travelled along the road. Paul probably saw it when he passed through here on his way from Neapolis, present-day Kavala, to Philippi.

Doubling back we pass the cemetery basilica again, and continue to walk to the west. Upon leaving Krenides we immediately find ourselves standing in front of the Neapolis Gate, the entrance to ancient Philippi. On our right-hand side we see the theatre. Behind the theatre, at a distance of about 100 metres to the north and to the northeast, we see several bas-relief sculptures in the stone wall of the acropolis. Most of these figures represent the goddess Diana. These works of art are dated to the second century CE.

The theatre is dated to the fourth century BCE. Some remnants from that time may still be seen today. The Romans expanded the theatre in the second century CE, adapting it to their requirements. Leaving the theatre we keep to the pavement for a few minutes, which will lead us to the sanctuary of Silvanus, just above the pavement. Long lists of names have been incised into the rocks. They are dated to the second and the third centuries. We are now very close to the northeast corner of Basilica A. This church is easily recognized by its outlines. The foundation of the pulpit is still there. Surviving parts of the wall show the original painting. This church was constructed around the year 500.

To the west of Basilica A we can see another church, Basilica C. This church was built at the beginning of the sixth century. It is not open to the public, but we can get a good impression by walking around it. The remnants of its two pulpits are visible as well.

If we continue our walk we will arrive at the museum. It is now open to the public again after many years of restoration. Many stones with interesting inscriptions have been erected in the museum garden. They are certainly worth a visit. Taking the path near the museum that zigzags to the top of the acropolis and continuing for about 150 metres, we find another collection of sculptures in the rock. About 20 of these are easy to spot as they are directly next to the path. Only 50 metres further on we see a chiselled cross in the stone; see Chapter 7 of this volume. If we climb to the top we can find still more sculptures.

Going down, we cross the secondary road south of Basilica A. This road was closed to traffic some years ago. A ring road around the excavation area, to the south of the old city walls, was completed several years before it was opened to traffic. The delay was caused by new archaeological finds. After crossing the road that runs below Basilica A we descend the stairs to arrive at the Via Egnatia; see Chapter 1 of this volume. Immediately in front of us lies the forum, surrounded by the ruins of Roman temples and administration buildings. Stones of different sizes bearing inscriptions are scattered over the area. Some inscriptions have not even been published yet. The inscriptions discussed in this book are only a tiny percentage of the over 800 that have been published.

Further south we see the enormous ruins of Basilica B; see Chapter 8 of this volume. The area of the Palaestra, the Roman institute for physical exercise, was used for the construction of this church. The centre of the nave is occupied by the apse of a later, smaller church. The most spectacular remains of the Palaestra are the well-preserved public latrines in the southeast corner (Figure 38). We return to the forum and go east along the Via Egnatia. A fence separates the eastern part of the excavation area from the forum. This area is sometimes closed in the afternoons. A part of the floor of the Basilica of Paul is visible, including the inscription that mentions Bishop Porphyrius. The floor of the Octagon, which was built about a century later, may be easily distinguished from the earlier floor of the Basilica by the difference in height. On the basis of these floors and other remnants we can establish the outlines of the successive churches that were built here. The apse is beautifully reconstructed.

The annexes to the Octagon include the splendid baptistery whose wall was pulled down. In Chapter 6 I argued that this wall was reconstructed a little further to the north with the purpose of attaining a square room for the baptistery. The diaconicon accommodates the water reservoir where the water was turned into holy water by the proximity of relics. Parts of the water pipe system may still be seen. The bath house is located to the north.

The area further to the east is closed. Students of archaeology of the Aristotle University of Thessaloniki come here for a couple of weeks each year to take part in the excavations under the direction of their teachers. But the activities progress extremely slowly. There are future plans to excavate a part of the western area of Philippi under the auspices of the Ministry of Culture, but it is impossible to tell when these excavations will start or when the first results will be published.

Book of Acts

16.11 We set sail from Troas and took a straight course to Samothrace, the following day to Neapolis, 12 and from there to Philippi, which is a leading city of the district of Macedonia and a Roman colony. We remained in this city for some days. 13 On the sabbath day we went outside the gate by the river, where we presumed there was a place of prayer; and we sat down and spoke to the women who had gathered there. 14 A certain woman named Lydia, a worshipper of God, was listening to us; she was from the city of Thyatira and a dealer in purple cloth. The Lord opened her heart to listen eagerly to what was said by Paul. 15 When she and her household were baptised, she urged us, saying, 'If you have judged me to be faithful to the Lord, come and stay at my home.' And she prevailed upon us.

16 One day, as we were going to the place of prayer, we met a slave girl who had a spirit of divination and brought her owners a great deal of money by fortune telling. 17 While she followed Paul and us, she would cry out, 'These men are slaves of the Most High God, who proclaim to you a way of salvation.' 18 She kept doing this for many days. But Paul, very much annoyed, turned and said to the spirit, 'I order you in the name of Jesus Christ to come out of her.' And it came out that very hour.

19 But when their owners saw that their hope of making money was gone, they seized Paul and Silas and dragged them into the marketplace before the authorities. 20 When they had brought them before the magistrates, they said, 'These men are disturbing our city; they are Jews 21 and are advocating customs that are not lawful for us as Romans to adopt or observe.' 22 The crowd joined in attacking them, and the magistrates had them stripped of their clothing and ordered them to be beaten with rods. 23 After they had given them a severe flogging, they threw them into prison and ordered the goaler to keep them securely. 24 Following these

instructions, he put them in the innermost cell and fastened their feet in the stocks.

25 About midnight Paul and Silas were praying and singing hymns to God, and the prisoners were listening to them. 26 Suddenly there was an earthquake, so violent that the foundations of the prison were shaken; and immediately all the doors were opened and everyone's chains were unfastened. 27 When the goaler woke up and saw the prison doors wide open, he drew his sword and was about to kill himself, since he supposed that the prisoners had escaped. 28 But Paul shouted in a loud voice, 'Do not harm yourself, for we are all here.' 29 The goaler called for lights, and rushing in, he fell down trembling before Paul and Silas. 30 Then he brought them outside and said, 'Sirs, what must I do to be saved?' 31 They answered, 'Believe in the Lord Jesus, and you will be saved, you and your household.' 32 They spoke the word of the Lord to him and to all who were in his house. 33 At the same hour of the night he took them and washed their wounds; then he and his entire family were baptised without delay. 34 He brought them up into the house and set food before them; and he and his entire household rejoiced that he had become a believer in God.

35 When morning came, the magistrates sent the police, saying, 'Let those men go.' 36 And the goaler reported the message to Paul, saying, 'The magistrates sent word to let you go; therefore come out now and go in peace.' 37 But Paul replied, 'They have beaten us in public, uncondemned, men who are Roman citizens, and have thrown us into prison; and now are they going to discharge us in secret? Certainly not! Let them come and take us out themselves.' 38 The police reported these words to the magistrates, and they were afraid when they heard that they were Roman citizens; 39 so they came and apologized to them. And they took them out and asked them to leave the city. 40 After leaving the prison they went to Lydia's home; and when they had seen and encouraged the brothers and sisters there, they departed.

17.1 After Paul and Silas had passed through Amphipolis and Apollonia, they came to Thessalonica, where there was a synagogue of the Jews.

20.1 After the uproar had ceased, Paul sent for the disciples; and after encouraging them and saying farewell, he left for Macedonia. 2 When he had gone through those regions and had given the believers much encouragement, he came to Greece, 3 where he stayed for three months. He was about to sail for Syria when a plot was made against him by the Jews, and so he decided to return through Macedonia. 4 He was accompanied by Sopater son of Pyrrhus from Beroea, by Aristarchus and Secundus from Thessalonica, by Gaius from Derbe, and by Timothy, as well as by Tychicus and Trophimus from Asia. 5 They went ahead and were waiting for us in Troas; but we sailed from Philippi after the days of Unleavened Bread, and in five days we joined them in Troas, where we stayed for seven days.

The Epistle of Paul to the Philippians

1.1 Paul and Timothy, servants of Christ Jesus, to all the saints in Christ Jesus who are in Philippi, with the bishops and deacons: *2* Grace to you and peace from God our Father and the Lord Jesus Christ.

3 I thank my God every time I remember you, *4* constantly praying with joy in every one of my prayers for all of you, *5* because of your sharing in the Gospel from the first day until now. *6* I am confident of this, that the one who began a good work among you will bring it to completion by the day of Jesus Christ. *7* It is right for me to think this way about all of you, because you hold me in your heart, for all of you share in God's grace with me, both in my imprisonment and in the defence and confirmation of the Gospel. *8* For God is my witness, how I long for all of you with the compassion of Christ Jesus. *9* And this is my prayer, that your love may overflow more and more with knowledge and full insight *10* to help you determine what is best, so that in the day of Christ you may be pure and blameless, *11* having produced the harvest of righteousness that comes through Jesus Christ for the glory and praise of God.

12 I want you to know, beloved that what has happened to me has actually helped to spread the Gospel, *13* so that it has become known throughout the whole imperial guard and to everyone else that my imprisonment is for Christ; *14* and most of the brothers and sisters, having been made confident in the Lord by my imprisonment, dare to speak the word with greater boldness and without fear.

15 Some proclaim Christ from envy and rivalry, but others from goodwill. *16* These proclaim Christ out of love, knowing that I have been put here for the defence of the Gospel; *17* the others proclaim Christ out of selfish ambition, not sincerely but intending to increase my suffering in my imprisonment. *18* What does it matter? Just this, that Christ is proclaimed in every way, whether out of false motives or true; and in that I rejoice. Yes, and I will continue to rejoice, *19* for I know that through your prayers and the help of the Spirit of Jesus Christ this will turn out for my deliverance. *20* It is my eager expectation and hope that I will not be put to shame in any way, but that by my speaking with all boldness, Christ will be exalted now as always in my body, whether by life or by death. *21* For to me, living is Christ and dying is gain. *22* If I am to live in the flesh, that means fruitful labour for me; and I do not know which I prefer. *23* I am hard pressed between the two; my desire is to depart and be with Christ, for that is far better; *24* but to remain in the flesh is more necessary for you. *25* Since I am convinced of this, I know that I will remain and continue with all of you for your progress and joy in faith, *26* so that I may share abundantly in your boasting in Christ Jesus when I come to you again.

27 Only, live your life in a manner worthy of the Gospel of Christ, so that, whether I come and see you or am absent and hear about you, I will know that you are standing firm in one spirit, striving side by side with one mind for the faith of the Gospel, *28* and are in no way intimidated by your opponents. For them this is evidence of their destruction, but of your salvation. And this is God's doing. *29* For he has graciously granted you the privilege not only of believing in Christ, but of suffering for him as well – *30* since you are having the same struggle that you saw I had and now hear that I still have.

2.1 If then there is any encouragement in Christ, any consolation from love, any sharing in the Spirit, any compassion and sympathy, *2* make my joy complete: be of the same mind, having the same love, being in full accord and of one mind. *3* Do nothing from selfish ambition or conceit, but in humility regard others as better than yourselves. *4* Let each of you look not to your own interests, but to the interests of others. *5* Let the same mind be in you that was in Christ Jesus,
6 who, though he was in the form of God,
did not regard equality with God
as something to be exploited,
7 but emptied himself,
taking the form of a slave,

being born in human likeness.
And being found in human form,
8 he humbled himself
and became obedient to the point of death –
even death on a cross.

9 Therefore God also highly exalted him
and gave him the name
that is above every name,
10 so that at the name of Jesus
every knee should bend,
in heaven and on earth,
11 and every tongue should confess
that Jesus Christ is Lord,
to the glory of God the Father.

12 Therefore, my beloved, just as you have always obeyed me, not only in my presence, but much more now in my absence, work out your own salvation with fear and trembling; 13 for it is God who is at work in you, enabling you both to will and to work for his good pleasure.

14 Do all things without murmuring and arguing, 15 so that you may be blameless and innocent, children of God without blemish in the midst of a crooked and perverse generation, in which you shine like stars in the world. 16 It is by your holding fast to the word of life that I can boast on the day of Christ that I did not run in vain or labour in vain. 17 But even if I am poured out as a libation over the sacrifice and the offering of your faith, I am glad and rejoice with all of you – 18 and in the same way you also must be glad and rejoice with me.

19 I hope in the Lord Jesus to send Timothy to you soon, so that I may be cheered by news of you. 20 I have no one like him who will be genuinely concerned for your welfare. 21 All of them are seeking their own interests, not those of Jesus Christ. 22 But Timothy's worth you know, how like a son with a father he has served with me in the work of the Gospel. 23 I hope therefore to send him as soon as I see how things go with me; 24 and I trust in the Lord that I will also come soon.

25 Still, I think it necessary to send to you Epaphroditus – my brother and co-worker and fellow soldier, your messenger and

minister to my need; 26 for he has been longing for all of you, and has been distressed because you heard that he was ill. 27 He was indeed so ill that he nearly died. But God had mercy on him, and not only on him but on me also, so that I would not have one sorrow after another. 28 I am the more eager to send him, therefore, in order that you may rejoice at seeing him again, and that I may be less anxious. 29 Welcome him then in the Lord with all joy, and honour such people, 30 because he came close to death for the work of Christ, risking his life to make up for those services that you could not give me.

3.1 Finally, my brothers and sisters, rejoice in the Lord. To write the same things to you is not troublesome to me, and for you it is a safeguard.

2 Beware of the dogs, beware of the evil workers, beware of those who mutilate the flesh! 3 For it is we who are the circumcision, who worship in the Spirit of God and boast in Christ Jesus and have no confidence in the flesh – 4 even though I, too, have reason for confidence in the flesh.

If anyone else has reason to be confident in the flesh, I have more: 5 circumcised on the eighth day, a member of the people of Israel, of the tribe of Benjamin, a Hebrew born of Hebrews; as to the law, a Pharisee; 6 as to zeal, a persecutor of the church; as to righteousness under the law, blameless.

7 Yet whatever gains I had, these I have come to regard as loss because of Christ. 8 More than that, I regard everything as loss because of the surpassing value of knowing Christ Jesus my Lord. For his sake I have suffered the loss of all things, and I regard them as rubbish, in order that I may gain Christ 9 and be found in him, not having a righteousness of my own that comes from the law, but one that comes through faith in Christ, the righteousness from God based on faith. 10 I want to know Christ and the power of his resurrection and the sharing of his sufferings by becoming like him in his death, 11 if somehow I may attain the resurrection from the dead.

12 Not that I have already obtained this or have already reached the goal; but I press on to make it my own, because Christ Jesus has made me his own. 13 Beloved, I do not consider that I have made it my own; but this one thing I do: forgetting what lies behind and straining forward to what lies ahead, 14 I press on towards the goal for the prize of the heavenly call of God in Christ Jesus. 15 Let

those of us then who are mature be of the same mind; and if you think differently about anything, this too God will reveal to you. 16 Only let us hold fast to what we have attained.

17 Brothers and sisters, join in imitating me, and observe those who live according to the example you have in us. 18 For many live as enemies of the cross of Christ; I have often told you of them, and now I tell you even with tears. 19 Their end is destruction; their god is the belly; and their glory is in their shame; their minds are set on earthly things. 20 But our citizenship is in heaven, and it is from there that we are expecting a Saviour, the Lord Jesus Christ. 21 He will transform the body of our humiliation that it may be conformed to the body of his glory, by the power that also enables him to make all things subject to himself. 4.1 Therefore, my brothers and sisters, whom I love and long for, my joy and crown, stand firm in the Lord in this way, my beloved.

2 I urge Euodia and I urge Syntyche to be of the same mind in the Lord. 3 Yes, and I ask you also, my loyal companion, help these women, for they have struggled beside me in the work of the Gospel, together with Clement and the rest of my co-workers, whose names are in the book of life.

4 Rejoice in the Lord always; again I will say, Rejoice. 5 Let your gentleness be known to everyone. The Lord is near. 6 Do not worry about anything, but in everything by prayer and supplication with thanksgiving let your requests be made known to God. 7 And the peace of God, which surpasses all understanding, will guard your hearts and your minds in Christ Jesus.

8 Finally, beloved, whatever is true, whatever is honourable, whatever is just, whatever is pure, whatever is pleasing, whatever is commendable, if there is any excellence and if there is anything worthy of praise, think about these things. 9 Keep on doing the things that you have learned and received and heard and seen in me, and the God of peace will be with you.

10 I rejoice in the Lord greatly that now at last you have revived your concern for me: indeed, you were concerned for me, but had no opportunity to show it. 11 Not that I am referring to being in need; for I have learned to be content with whatever I have. 12 I know what it is to have little, and I know what it is to have plenty. In any and all circumstances I have learned the secret of being well fed and of going hungry, of having plenty and of being in need. 13

I can do all things through him who strengthens me. *14* In any case, it was kind of you to share my distress.

15 You Philippians indeed know that in the early days of the gospel, when I left Macedonia, no church shared with me in the matter of giving and receiving, except you alone. *16* For even when I was in Thessalonica, you sent me help for my needs more than once. *17* Not that I seek the gift, but I seek the profit that accumulates to your account. *18* I have been paid in full and have more than enough; I am fully satisfied, now that I have received from Epaphroditus the gifts you sent, a fragrant offering, a sacrifice acceptable and pleasing to God. *19* And my God will fully satisfy every need of yours according to his riches in glory in Christ Jesus. *20* To our God and Father be glory forever and ever. Amen.

21 Greet every saint in Christ Jesus. The friends who are with me greet you. *22* All the saints greet you, especially those of the Emperor's household.

23 The grace of the Lord Jesus Christ be with your spirit.

BIBLIOGRAPHY

This bibliography contains only a small selection of the available literature. Exhaustive bibliographies may be found in the books by Peter Pilhofer, which are included in this list.

The following two books are quite old, but are invaluable to scholars who study Philippi in any detail:

Paul Collart, *Philippes. Ville de Macédoine depuis ses origines jusqu'à la fin de l'époque romaine* I–II. Paris: E. de Boccard, 1937.
Paul Lemerle, *Philippes et la Macédoine orientale à l'époque chrétienne et byzantine* I–II. Bibliothèque des écoles Françaises d' Athènes et de Rome 158. Paris: E. de Boccard, 1945.

The sculptures at the acropolis are brilliantly mapped and discussed in:

Paul Collart, Pierre Ducrey, *Philippes I. Les reliefs rupestres*. Bulletin de correspondance Hellénique, Supplément II. Paris: Boccard, 1975.

The comprehensive studies by Peter Pilhofer are the most important books from the modern literature:

Peter Pilhofer, *Philippi I. Die erste christliche Gemeinde Europas*. Wissenschaftliche Untersuchungen zum Neuen Testament 87. Tübingen: Mohr, 1995.
—*Philippi II. Katalog der Inschriften von Philippi*. Wissenschaftliche Untersuchungen zum Neuen Testament 119.2, überarbeitete und ergänzte Auflage. Tübingen: Mohr, 2009.

In addition to these studies I would like to mention the following:

V. A. Abrahamsen, *Women and Worship at Philippi*. Portland: Astarte Shell, 1995.
C. Bakirtzis and H. Koester (eds), *Philippi at the Time of Paul and after His Death*. Harrisburg: Trinity, 1998.

L. Bormann, *Philippi, Stadt und Christengemeinde zur Zeit des Paulus.* Supplements to Novum Testamentum 78. Leiden: Brill, 1995.

W. Elliger, *Mit Paulus unterwegs in Griechenland.* Stuttgart: Katholisches Bibelwerk, 1998.

C. Koukouli-Chrysanthaki and C. Bakirtzis, *Philippi.* Athens: Ministry of Culture, 1995.

P. Oakes, *Philippians.* Society for New Testament Studies. Monograph Series 110. Cambridge: University Press, 2001.

L. Portefaix, *Sisters Rejoice. Paul's Letter to the Philippians and Luke-Acts as seen by First-century Philippian Women.* Coniectanea Biblica, New Testament Series 20. Stockholm: Almqvist & Wiksell, 1988.

R. Stark, *The Rise of Christianity.* San Francisco, CA: Harper, 1996.

M. Tellbe, *Paul between Synagogue and State.* Coniectanea Biblica, New Testament Series 34. Stockholm: Almqvist & Wiksell, 2001.

E. Verhoef, 'Syzygos' in Phil 4:3 and the author of the 'We-sections' in Acts, *Journal of Higher Criticism* 5/2 (1998), 209–19.

—The Church of Philippi in the first six centuries of our era, *Teologiese Studies* 61/1 and 2 (2005), 565–92.

—Syncretism in the church of Philippi, *Teologiese Studies* 63/3 (2008), 697–714.

C. S. de Vos, *Church and Community Conflicts.* SBL Dissertation Series 168. Atlanta: Scholars Press, 1997.

With regard to the Epistle of Paul to the Philippians, the following books deserve mention:

J. Reumann, *Philippians.* The Anchor Yale Bible 33B. New Haven, CT: Yale University Press, 2008.

M. Silva, *Philippians.* Baker Exegetical Commentary on the New Testament. Grand Rapids: Baker, 1992.

E. Verhoef, *Filippenzen. Filemon.* Tekst en Toelichting. Kampen: Kok, 1998 (Dutch).

For the epistle of Polycarp to the Philippians, see:

W. Bauer and H. Paulsen, *Die Briefe des Ignatius von Antiochia und der Polykarpbrief.* Handbuch zum Neuen Testament 18.II. Tübingen: Mohr, 1985.

The excavations in Philippi are annually reported in the Greek journals *Praktika* and *Archailogikon Deltion.* Their progress is also regularly discussed in the French series *Bulletin de correspondance Hellénique.* In

2004 G. Gounaris, then Professor of Archaeology at the University of Thessaloniki, published a Greek guide:

G. G. Gounaris and E. Gounari, *Philippoi. Archaiologikos odigos.* Thessaloniki: University Studio Press, 2004. An English edition was published simultaneously by the same publisher: *Philippi: Archaeological Guide.*

A French guide was published recently:

M. Sève and P. Weber, *Guide du forum de Philippes.* Sites et monuments 18. Athens: École Française d'Athènes, 2012.

INDEX OF BIBLICAL REFERENCES

Texts from Philippians and from Acts that are mentioned in Chapters 2 and 3 are not listed here.

INDEX

'Philippi' and 'Paul' are not included in this index, because they are mentioned on practically every page. Names that are mentioned in passing are not included either.